Feminine, Free and Faithful

Feminine, Free and Faithful

by
RONDA CHERVIN

IGNATIUS PRESS   SAN FRANCISCO

Contents

Introduction

I believe that within all women there is a deep desire to be feminine. With rare exceptions, women prefer to be considered warm not cold, charming not repressed, and wise not merely critical.

I believe that within all women there is also a deep desire to be free: a desire to be daring and spontaneous rather than frightened and stiff; to be strong and initiating, not weak and dependent; to be objective and rational, not unrealistic and irrational.

I believe that being faithful to God is the key to unfolding the feminine and free personality. The faithful woman has the strength to use her feminine gifts for the good of the Kingdom that Christ came to form "on earth as it is in heaven". The faithful woman has the love that enables her to use her freedom for the good of everyone she encounters.

My experiences have been both the source and the impetus for writing *Feminine, Free and Faithful*. I am a wife and the mother of two young women (twins) and a teenage son. A professor of philosophy, I teach courses in the philosophy of woman. A convert to Catholicism, I come from a Jewish, though atheistic, background. I am a writer, speaker, workshop and retreat leader and one of the five women consultants to the United States Bishops who are writing a pastoral on the concerns of women.

In 1980 I coauthored *The Woman's Tale* with Sister Mary Neill, O.P.; it is an imaginative book that uses the female characters of the fairy tales to help women explore their own personal journeys. Since the time that book was written, issues about women in society and in the Church have become even more controversial.

As a consultant to the Bishops I daily hear the opinions of Catholic women: they voice all sides and manners, from impulsive cries to polished manifestos. Lately I have noticed a false alternative developing: either women should be feminine and forget about liberation *or* women should be liberated and realize that "femininity" is a euphemism for slavery. Generally those in the profeminine contingent believe in absolute adherence to the teachings of the Church, and those in the proliberation contingent think there is plenty of room for creative change.

The growing division of Catholic women into these two groups troubles me. I had always thought that women could be feminine and free, and that loving fidelity to the teachings of the Church was not a hindrance, but the necessary condition for creative growth. I wrote the first version of this book, "Feminine and Free", to *prove* that there was a way to avoid false alternatives.

However, while using my book in courses at catechetical institutes and seminaries and in workshops at retreat houses, I realized that intellectual clarity must be balanced by personal healing in the areas of the feminine and masculine. And so in this, my final version, I have combined facts and concepts with suggestions for individual appropriation.

Although *Feminine, Free and Faithful* is written primarily for women, I have found that many men also consider it an important book. It can be an aid to understanding the teachings of the Church and to realizing the masculine ambivalence toward women which is encountered in daily life.

This chapter will introduce you to the ideas developed in *Feminine, Free and Faithful* in a unique way. In it I have shared my own experiences of being feminine, free and faithful, and I have provided an opportunity for you to consider your experiences as well. In the first portion of the book, devoted to femininity, we will explore positive and negative feminine traits. We will investigate the roots of such characteristics with reference to biological, psychological and sociological viewpoints. Then we will consider the theory of *complementarity*, which tries to show that feminine and masculine traits are intrinsic and that they fit men and women in a way that reflects how they are to relate to one another. Next the theological foundations for the Church's teaching on the feminine, including major consequences in ethics, are presented; and the chapter ends with suggestions for healing prayer.

The chapter on "Freedom" considers the difference between freedom from oppression and liberty to be oneself in the service of God. Consideration of elements of freedom such as spontaneity, daring, strength, leadership and objectivity shows that these traits are compatible with femininity and faithfulness. Protests concerning language and the roles of women in the Church are evaluated, and femininism and the Jungian theory of wholeness are analyzed in their positive and negative aspects. This chapter also concludes with possibilities for healing prayer.

Both chapters address women in the single, married and consecrated life. Further, they highlight Mary, the

Mother of God, and the women saints as our "fore-mothers" and heroines, for surely in these women we have tangible proof that being a woman of faith means being both feminine and free.

Now that you have a better idea of what you will find in pages to come, take this opportunity to make this study more personal by answering some key questions. I will give my response and you can answer either mentally or in a notebook. Sharing this with another person or in a group is often very helpful.

— *When have you felt most feminine?* The occasions when I feel most feminine would include when receiving the male sexual explosion of energy, especially when there is hope of new life, experiencing pregnancy, and breast feeding and enjoying the beauty of my children. I would also include those times when my relentless mind comes to rest and I can simply enjoy the presence of others; when I can flow with love for family, friends or God.

— *When has femininity seemed most like a trap?* I feel this way when some traditional feminine duty interferes with my natural inclinations, for example, when I have to remove dishes from the table just when I want to hear what a guest will say next, or when I must respond to a child's needs just when I am at a peak in my writing. I also feel angry when my ideas are dismissed because I am a woman and therefore considered unimportant. While this is rarer nowadays, it is nonetheless annoying when it does occur.

— *When do you feel most free?* I feel freest when I am spontaneous in a usually formal situation. It gives me enormous joy when, in the middle of a philosophy class, I think of a creative way to improve the situation and immediately put it into practice. I also feel free when someone shows me that I am loved for myself and not for some set image or a beneficial role I can play.

— *When does your own freedom feel most dangerous to your welfare or that of others?* I feel terrified when I see that some whimsical stance, born of insecurity, alienates me from others, leaving me in the cold. I am consumed with guilt when I realize that some wild decision of mine could bring about permanent harm to myself or my loved ones.

— *When do you feel most feminine, free and faithful?* I can be all of these when living out the truths of the Catholic faith. At daily Mass I feel feminine because I am in a yearning, surrendering interior posture. I feel free because I choose to center my soul on God in this manner. I am faithful because I am taken up in awe of my Lord's great gesture of love in sacrificing himself for me and entering my very body each day. I also can be feminine, free and faithful when I am being loving to my husband and children, especially by openly expressed affection. (Doing chores feels less free.) When lecturing or ministering to a receptive group of Christians I feel most feminine, free and faithful as the Holy Spirit moves through me so that doctrines of the Church glow with mystical fire.

— *Who are women you have known or read about who seem to embody femininity, freedom, faithfulness or all three?* For feminine warmth I think of my mother who never let her children go to sleep without a hug and whose bed was an ever-available refuge. For feminine gracefulness I think of my twin sister, a dancer, whose ethereal, beautiful movements enchant me. For freedom I think of unconventional heroines such as Emily Dickinson,

Caryll Houselander, Flannery O'Connor. Women who are feminine, free and faithful include Mary and my favorite saints who are like spiritual sisters to me: Mary Magdalen, Catherine of Siena, Teresa of Avila and Thérèse of Lisieux, Elizabeth Ann Seton and modern-day women such as Adrienne von Speyr, Alice von Hildebrand and Mother Teresa of Calcutta.

While writing *Feminine, Free and Faithful*, my prayer has been that this book may help me as well as you to develop the best qualities of femininity and freedom as faithful daughters of the Church.

Femininity

This chapter begins with a list of traits that many consider to be feminine. You will decide how many of these qualities you have. Then we focus on particular key positive traits and their negative opposites:

> warmth versus coldness or smothering
> charm versus repression or seduction
> intuitiveness versus over-criticalness or subjectivism

We will see how biologists, psychologists, sociologists and philosophers explain the roots of such traditionally feminine traits. The pros and cons of the theory of complementarity, which claims that femininity and masculinity are intrinsic to women and men, will be analyzed. Finally, the feminine as transfigured by faith will be explored both from a doctrinal and a spiritual point of view.

Feminine Traits

Below is a list of qualities. Check the ones you think you have and circle the ones you wish you had to a greater degree. If you wish to pass this book on to another reader you can make your own separate list.

capable	polite
catty	pouty
charming	prudish
chatter-box	pure
compassionate	quiet
complaining	receptive
considerate	responsive
delicate	seductive
diplomatic	sensitive
empathetic	sensually receptive
enduring	sentimental
expressive	silly
faithful	sincere
fearful	slavish
flirtatious	smothering
gentle	spiritual
graceful	spiteful
hospitable	supportive
hysterical	sweet
intuitive	tender
manipulative	trusting
modest	vain
moody	vulnerable
nagging	warm
naive	weak
obedient	weepy
passive	wise
perceptive	wishy-washy
petty	

Later, in our healing prayer section, we will return to this list of traits so that you may work with it further. For now, I will simply state that most participants in my workshops on the feminine have considered the following characteristics to be positive feminine traits:

Positive Feminine Traits

responsive, compassionate, empathetic, enduring, gentle, warm, tender, hospitable, receptive, diplomatic, considerate, polite, supportive, intuitive, wise, perceptive, sensitive, spiritual, sincere, vulnerable (in the sense of emotionally open), obedient, trusting, graceful, sweet, expressive, charming, delicate, quiet, sensually receptive (vs. prudish), faithful, pure

Here are some well-known women from history, literature and contemporary life who exhibit many of these positive feminine traits: Ruth, Naomi, Sarah, Saint Anne, Saint Elizabeth, Mary the Mother of God, Saint Gertrude, Saint Elizabeth of Hungary, Saint Thérèse of Lisieux, Saint Elizabeth Ann Seton and many other women saints, Cordelia of *King Lear*, Melanie in *Gone with the Wind*, Grace Kelly and Mother Teresa of Calcutta.

Men who possess many of these positive feminine traits are often considered to be fatherly. In a later section of this chapter, I will try to show why such designations are valid.

In my unofficial survey, most people consider the following to be negative feminine traits:

Negative Feminine Traits

weak, passive, slavish, weepy, wishy-washy, seductive, flirtatious, vain, chatter-box, silly, sentimental, naive, moody, petty, catty, prudish, manipulative, complaining, nagging, pouty, smothering, spiteful

Famous women who manifest some of these negative traits include: Delilah, Salome, Herodias, Medea, Cleopatra, Ophelia, Margaret of Goethe's *Faust*, Madame Butterfly, Anna Karenina, Grushenka of *The Brothers Karamazov*, Scarlet O'Hara, Elizabeth Taylor, Marilyn Monroe, Blanche of *A Streetcar Named Desire*, Jean Harris, Dolly Parton's usual roles, Lucy of "I Love Lucy", Edith Bunker of "All in the Family", Alexis in "Dynasty".

Shakespeare put in the mouth of Iago, the villain of *Othello*, this derisive description of the feminine:

> You are pictures out of doors
> belles in your parlours
> wild cats in your kitchens
> saints in your injuries
> devils being offended
> players at housewifery
> and housewives in your beds.

Men are usually called effeminate if they have developed negative feminine traits. A man with positive feminine traits might be considered gentle or soft but usually not effeminate. Some examples of effeminate men would be Peter Ustinov's portrayal of Nero in *Quo Vadis*, Oscar Wilde, Truman Capote and Boy George. You can probably think of some others.

THE NATURE OF FEMININE TRAITS

This section concentrates on three clusters of feminine traits: warmth, charm and intuitiveness.

A warm woman exhibits a combination of traits:

responsiveness, compassion, empathy, endurance, gentleness, tenderness, hospitality, receptivity, sensitivity, considerateness, politeness, supportiveness and faithfulness. Such a woman is said to be motherly, loving or, in modern parlance, nurturing.

Warmth is not only the opposite of coldness but also of that distortion of affection that is found in smothering, which includes negative feminine traits such as pettiness, manipulativeness, complaining, nagging, pouting and spitefulness.

Warmth is a response of love to the neediness of others. A woman who is empathetic and sensitive is highly aware of the vulnerability of others and reaches out to them.

In the single life, womanly warmth expresses itself in the family, in work situations, in the parish and community and in friendships with women and men. Married women lavish warmth primarily on their husbands and children. Consecrated religious women manifest warmth largely in prayer, in their community and in ministry.

Coldness comes from self-preoccupation: signals that others are in need do not reach the heart. This self-preoccupation usually springs from deep psychological causes, such as inadequate mothering, or from past experiences of feeling victimized by particular types of individuals, so that one may be cold toward one group yet warm toward others.

The need to smother usually results from an insecurity about oneself and others. Afraid of failure, such a woman surrounds others with her worried precautions, nags them to succeed and feels personally deflated when loved ones show their shortcomings. In the healing segment of this chapter, paths will be opened for overcoming such negative characteristics.

I view charm in its positive form as a composite of sweetness, gracefulness, expressiveness, delicacy, sensual receptivity and the emotional openness we call vulnerability.

Some consider charm to be a synonym for physical beauty, yet we all know women whose physical perfection seems plastic and stiff, and others who are not conventionally attractive yet who emanate charm. It is said that Alma Mahler, wife of Gustav Mahler, was a large, clumsy woman and yet charmed the very milkman at her door, even in her seventies!

A single woman exudes charm as a daughter and a sister in a family, in school, work and social life.

While a married woman may be especially charming with her husband and children, she is also charming with relatives, guests and people at work.

A woman religious becomes charming in her bridal relationship with Christ, as in the Song of Songs. This charm expresses itself in her relationships with others, not as a prelude to sexual intimacy, but as a delicate receptivity and appreciation or a warm unrepressed presence.

It is easy to see what charm is by considering its opposite, a repressed plainness. A locked-up woman is unresponsive, often bitter and resentful; she lacks the delicacy to appreciate what is loveable in others. Many repressed women are shy, which seems to exonerate them from blame. Yet psychologists show that shyness, while rooted in sad childhood circumstances, also demonstrates a self-absorbed fear of being hurt, an unwillingness to risk hurt in order to affirm others.

Charm in its negative form is called seductiveness. While the genuinely charming woman wants to show her responsiveness to others because she values them, the flirtatious or seductive woman wants the thrill of conquest. Often she does not even like sex very much. In contrast, the charming, sensually–receptive woman is aware of the attractiveness of others and indicates this by a sort of playfulness of positive warmth. The seductress is not concerned with the other person except as one who can confirm her own sexual value.

Usually healing in this area can come only with intensive counselling. The next section, which discusses the roots of positive and negative traits, will also provide insight.

The feminine trait of intuitiveness is rather controversial. It doesn't mean having hunches, but coming to a truth through a perceptiveness and a wisdom that is deeper than the analytic process.

Single women might demonstrate intuitiveness in their relationships within the family, at school, at work, in the parish community and in friendships. Often single women, because they are less burdened by family duties, will become informal or formal counselors, using their intuitive gifts to benefit others.

Married women greatly need intuition in their dealings with husband and children, because they must adapt general truths to their loved ones' individual characters.

Women religious need intuitive wisdom to respond to God revealed in his teachings and providence, lest they lose their faith through the influence of rationalistic trends.

Intuition is the opposite of overly critical, destructive reasoning. Intuition pierces to the center of reality, whereas the analytic process merely circles and takes jabs at it. But intuition is also opposite to subjectivity, in which emotion overtakes reason to yield biased or sentimental ideas instead of truth.

Again, in the section on healing and prayer we will see how such deformations might be overcome.

Now I will provide insights into the roots of feminine traits by considering theories from several different disciplines. It is important to cover these ideas in some detail, because the Christian feminist critique of some positions held by the Magisterium often assumes that natural knowledge does not substantiate Catholic concepts.

ROOTS OF THE FEMININE

Biological Features of the Feminine

Since I am a philosopher and spiritual writer and not a biologist, there is no way I can present a definitive analysis of the research, past and present, concerning the biology of the sexes. Nonetheless, it is important to consider some of these findings, for you will often hear references to the *merely* biological differences between men and women, as if these considerable differences had little relationship to the real masculine and feminine characteristics. I agree instead with those thinkers who hold that the physical differences are the manifestations as well as the causes of many psychological, intellectual and spiritual differences.

As you read this section you may want to make it more personal by pausing to consider how a particular fact or theory corresponds to your own thoughts and feelings as a woman.

In his massive study *Man and Woman in Christ*, the sociologist-philosopher-theologian Stephen B. Clark (1980, 200 and 719) has summarized the findings of biologists. Here are the key points concerning the differences between males and females:

— From birth on, males have more muscle than females.
— In any given population, the average male height and weight will exceed the female average.
— The human male is more susceptible to many diseases and birth defects.
— Females on the average live longer than males.
— Females mature earlier.
— The female hormonal system operates on a more cyclical pattern.
— Male and female brains differ.
— Males and females differ in sex organs, body hair and vocal pitch.

Some thinkers hold that greater physical strength naturally leads to dominance and aggressiveness as part of the male role of insuring the physical survival of the tribe. This may be indicated by studies of male primate behavior (Tiger and Fox 1971).

According to Darwin, men have stronger, bigger bodies and more muscular, wider shoulders as a result of natural selection, the survival of the fittest. Women differ from men just as mares differ from stallions. Man reacts to nature by attack and penetration; he fights animals and conquers forests. He is "against" nature. In contrast, woman is more in tune with nature because of her birthing cycles.

According to Freud, females are passive because they have less libido, or life energy. Women may be considered physically weaker because so much of their biological energy goes into reproductive functions: menstruation, childbearing and breast-feeding. Finally, man's sexual nature involves the aggressive thrust of the penis with the woman in a submissive posture.

Such findings, however, need not lead to the assumption that women are biologically inferior or secondary. According to Hans Urs von Balthasar in "Ephesians 5:21–33 and Humanae Vitae: A Meditation", in *Christian Married Love* (1981, 62):

> Competent biologists have expressed the view that the basic embryonic structure of all living beings, including man, is primarily feminine, and the subsequent differentiation of the male arises from a tendency toward extreme formations, while the development of the female shows a persistence in the original balance.

In an article by Jo Durden-Smith, "Male and Female—Why?", we find this surprising information: "A female fetus has two 'X' chromosomes. . . . The natural form of the human is female. It is the male's 'Y' chromosome that interferes with the natural development by causing production of something called $H - Y$ antigen. This coats the developing gonads . . . and forces them instead to become testicles . . . [that] pump out a hormone which absorbs the female structures that would have become the womb . . . and then they produce testosterone, which . . . causes the progressive reshaping of the male genitalia" (Durden-Smith in *The Collegiate Career Woman*, 1980).

Clearly, it is biased thinking to consider the strength to move boulders to be the model for physical prowess, and the ability to bear children to be an inferior function. The biological energy required by female functions might instead be considered to make her superior.

Relating this information to negative and positive feminine traits, one might say that relative muscular weakness is a root of the passivity of women in male/female relations. On the other hand, a woman's ability to bear children carries with it advantages for expressing the positive feminine traits of empathy and warmth. What is more, the greater delicacy of the feminine frame has a lot to do with positive traits of charm and evocation of the lyrical. Think of the beauty of the body of the ballerina as its graceful movements are supported by the male dancer.

Another biological feature that greatly affects feminine traits is the menstrual cycle. Karl Stern (1965), the psychiatrist, in *The Flight from Woman* considers it a positive feature of the female way of being to be tied to nature and unable to control it. He points out that "mother" and "matter" are related words and that because of her cycle woman has *time* in her own body in a deeper way than man does.

Women scholars in many fields tend to be interested in the ways the menstrual cycle contributes to the development of negative feminine traits. Differing energy levels throughout the cycle can lead to nervousness and moodiness. A woman is much more responsive in relationships and in work situations at certain times of her cycle than at others. The frequent presence of pain, often severe, during the menstrual flow, certainly causes many a woman to feel victimized by her sexuality and consequently she may be tempted to nag or lash out at the men in her environment (*see* Harding 1971).

The female experience of the sex act itself may also affect negative and positive feminine traits.

The woman's sexual organs are basically concave and

thus suitable to receive a convex object, the penis. While Karl Stern believes this phenomenon contributes positively to feminine receptivity, Simone de Beauvoir (1952), in *The Second Sex*, writes that the female's actual sexual shape is a symbol of humiliation and slavery. A foreign body can penetrate and enter her, but the male's experience of sex involves no such violation of his interiority. The male penis represents his agility and strength, while the woman's concavity represents her inferior immanence. She can only receive by waiting and then clinging, a negative posture, according to de Beauvoir.

In the sex act the woman provides a home for the male, even a symbolic return to the womb. On the other hand, a woman must be open to receive the power of the male's sexual entry.

Self-images of independent completeness and overly ambitious desires for fulfillment on her own terms may block a woman's experience of the joy in receiving the mysterious otherness of a man. Women who are puritanical about sex may be refusing to accept they have a female body, desiring to remain intact or hating to need others. The body is seen as a dirty, alien and uncontrollable thing.

Lesbianism may be related in part to a resentment toward this invasion by the dominant male, creating a preference for the equality of the mutual touch in female/female sexual relations. Masturbation, as a sexual lifestyle, could also be viewed in some cases as a bid for autonomy and as a means for avoiding the vulnerability that women feel in male/female sexual relations.

Some psychologists consider the very essence of female sexuality to be destined for reproduction rather than orgasm, however subjectively pleasurable the latter might be. Karl Stern thinks it is a woman's sexual nature to want to hold and envelop the male organ inside her just as she will eventually envelop the child. He finds the contemporary emphasis on female orgasm to be a masked form of frigidity.

It would seem self-evident that childbearing is the apex of the feminine experience of life. Yet in our society it has become almost peripheral, largely due to the contraceptive mentality. Our urban manner of living permits pregnancy to be almost a private event and militates against the consciousness of pregnancy as central to womanhood. Compare this to the vision a young girl would have of her own future were she living in a small village. There she would know of the birth of babies within a day, watch them being breast-fed and perhaps every few years count one new baby born to each fertile woman.

Here again we find a physical root of femininity contributing to both positive and negative traits.

Some of the most endearing womanly qualities stem, if not from the direct experience of pregnancy, at least from the potential for nurturing a tiny human in one's own body. Once the shock of finding oneself pregnant wears off and the morning sickness is over, a woman usually feels extremely tender and sweet toward the miniature person in her womb. There is no bond so strong, psychologists tell us, as that between a mother and her child. Many women who abort go through intense anguish at the time their baby would have been born had they carried to term (Stern 1965). The child is a part of the mother, observed the writer Gertrud von Le Fort (1962), and the mother can feel this being "part of" as something blissful. "Loss" of such oneness accounts for the sadness of postpartum depression.

I recall that, in spite of extreme morning sickness due

to a twin pregnancy and fear of yet another miscarriage, I was euphoric in my sense of self during that pregnancy. Proud, dreamy and content, I walked around as if bearing the Savior. Such memories ratify the statement of Karl Stern (1965) in *The Flight from Woman* that the sense of the *infinite importance of the individual* is rooted in the experience of pregnancy, birth and nursing. Every birth is a nativity, a cooperation with God's basic act of creation. A woman develops the warmth of her character as she cherishes her unique baby. As von Hildebrand thought, "children are the love of the couple made visible" (von Hildebrand 1965, cf. 91–93).

During my last pregnancy, in my middle thirties, this joy reached its peak. Since I had already fulfilled my career goals, I was better able to enter into the mysterious meaning of life itself, which transcended all exterior aims.

I wondered if my previous ambitions had made me too masculine so that I could not fully enjoy my first experiences of motherhood. Surely, the insight into the masculine world afforded me by my career helped me understand Darwin's idea that women had become more tender and less selfish because of their maternal instincts, while men had become less warm since they had to rival other men. Men had learned to find their delight in competition. Did Darwin's ideas also explain why men spend their weekends in front of the TV set watching other men compete at sports?

In "Male and Female—Why?" Durden-Smith provides a sociological perspective:

> For 99% of human history, we've lived as hunter gatherers. The men have been hunters, loners, requiring pronounced visual skills and goal-direction. The women

have lived together in groups with children and the old. So it seems to me evolutionarily adaptive that women have acquired different abilities—social, acculturative, nurturant ones that men, by and large, don't have. . . . This implies a sexual stamping, a generic one . . . in the brain . . . in the fetus . . . reinforced and magnified by our cultural institutions (Durden-Smith 1980, 14).

So far the writers quoted have emphasized the positive feminine traits that result from the uniquely female ability to bear children in the womb. What about the other side? Simone de Beauvoir, in *The Second Sex*, sees pregnancy as a symbolic enslavement and the child as a sort of parasite gnawing away at the mother's strength. For de Beauvoir the maternal instinct should not be glorified, for it is truly a mixture of many emotions. Perhaps the experience of being a victim of one's own bodily inheritance can partially explain such negative traits as being self-pitying, weepy, complaining, nagging and spiteful. This behavior may also be a woman's way of getting even with the impregnating male, who is physically free of the burden of his fertility.

Let's return to the positive experience of the female body and its potentialities. The word "bonding" is being used to describe the link that forms between mother and child during pregnancy and that continues after birth. Many women believe that breast-feeding is part of this bonding process. The hormones that a mother builds up during pregnancy prepare her for breast-feeding and other maternal responses, as indicated in many studies. Breast-feeding, however, has not always been popular in our society. In the beginning of the industrial era, when it became profitable to hire women for factory work, breast-feeding went out of style and the invention of the bottle was considered a wonderful advance. In our times breast-feeding is on the upswing. Studies show that human milk is healthy for the baby. The sensual, emotional and spiritual joys a mother experiences by breast-feeding, as well as the great importance of the bond that nursing creates between the baby and the mother, are being emphasized.

Such physical aspects of mothering affect the development of positive feminine traits. A study of female rats showed an interesting change in behavior: before giving birth, the rat preferred looking for food rather than staying with baby rats in the environment; after giving birth to her own babies, she would remain close to the babies rather than seek food. This could be seen as analogous to the willingness of human mothers to sacrifice for their children.

Some women find that their breasts ache when they imagine their infants are in trouble. Proponents of breast-feeding, such as members of La Leche League, hold that mothers have more empathy for the children they breast-fed than for those they fed with a bottle. An African word for mother means "she who hears when I call".

The psychologist Erik Erikson makes much of the fact that when girls play they want to shelter things in houses or to wrap them up; in contrast, boys are more interested in games involving exterior mobility.

The physical roots of feminine traits are not, however, limited to women who actually bear children in the womb. Women who adopt can be just as maternal as "birth" mothers, and so can single or celibate women. An explanation, which concurs with the theories of Karl Stern and others, would be that biological capabilities affect the whole psychology of a woman whether or not these capabilities are fulfilled.

Another reason all women can be maternal might be that the feminine figure is generally rounder and softer than the male figure. To be held by a woman gives one a feeling of sinking into *warmth*, of coming to refuge; being hugged by most men gives one a greater feeling of protective *strength*. Clothing that emphasizes a woman's breasts has a maternal, earthy appeal as well as a sexual one.

Of course, the same feminine figure can symbolize such negative feminine traits as smothering or promiscuous seductiveness, and such positive traits as beauty and delicacy. Many women are too close to their own bodies, or too intimidated by "perfect" fold-out images, to realize that men find the feminine body in itself attractive.

The fact that woman's genital sexual sphere is veiled and hidden, unlike a man's, contributes to the mysterious quality men find in women, claims Gertrud von Le Fort (1962) in *The Eternal Woman*. Such factors may heighten the sensual receptivity of women or lead to polar negative traits, a puritanic closedness at one extreme and coquettish attempts to trap a man at the other extreme.

What about brain differences between female and male and their effect on feminine traits such as silliness, being scatterbrained, petty, sensitive or intuitive? "Male and Female—Why?" summarizes recent studies on the nature of the brain and its hemispheres. These studies indicate that the left hemisphere of the brain, which specializes in visual tasks, mathematics, the perception of spatial relations and conceptualization, is more developed in most males than in the females. The more developed right brain of females makes them better at verbal skills and more sensitive to nuances. "Females are sensitive to context, good at picking up information that is incidental to a task that's set them, and distractible" (Durden-Smith 1980, 11–13). This makes them adept at reading emotions in faces and hearing nuances in voices. Such sensitivity can explain why women have so many observations to share when chatting. The appearance of silliness can belie the more deeply-rooted need to understand what is going on in personal situations.

While reading a Jane Austen novel, consisting mainly of conversations between women in a small English village, I was struck by this comparison: all the intellectual energy a contemporary woman devotes to a career, used to be expended in arranging daily life situations to insure the greatest comfort and pleasure. In the past, a woman worked to create a comfortable environment for her guests; even the character defects of her guests were mitigated by such strategies as well-planned seating arrangements or the subtle compliment. One wonders whether our contemporary need to get "high" as quickly as possible on social occasions is related to the lack of interest women now take in studying the intricacies of such social interaction. Naturally the same intuitive wisdom once employed for the comfort of others can be used to further selfish purposes as well.

It is often said that women are more intuitive because they combine heart and head more often than their male counterparts do, an idea which can be evaluated negatively or positively. For example, according to Karl Stern, the Spanish philosopher Ortega y Gasset thinks women are less rational and practical than men. Stern describes men as going around objects from the outside in an overly analytic manner, whereas women internalize, permitting reality to enter themselves and coming into intellectual sympathy with an object before drawing conclusions (Stern 1965, 25–26).

Sociological and Psychological Factors

Many battles are being fought between those who believe that negative feminine traits are caused solely by socio-logical and psychological reinforcement, largely in the interests of the male, and those who consider such feminine traits to be innate. In the opposite, less vitriolic, camp, we find those who argue that positive feminine traits are indeed largely dependent on reinforcement and that the growing lack of such support in our feminist climate is leading to the disappearance of some of the noblest qualities of the human race.

Much discussion concerns the concept of nurturing. Woman is seen as one who nurtures, who provides what is nourishing in the way of food and psychological support. In the past this quality was more simply desig-nated by the words "motherly", "maternal", or even more simply, "love". Thus Dante wrote that woman possesses the spirit of love. Lord Byron penned the fascinating lines in the poem *Don Juan*, "Man's love is of man's life a thing apart, 'Tis woman's whole existence. . . ."

A child learns to communicate inter-subjectively as he lies in the mother's arms receiving essential food and tenderness. A mother's experience of loving empathy with her needy, completely dependent child may lead her to view all human beings as children, who still need her food, her warmth, her compassion. And thus she becomes not only tender but also sensitive. This is why women ought to become nurses, teachers, social workers and even businesswomen, because they may bring their womanly love into such public situations.

Edith Stein attributes the ability to sense the value of the unique individual to the physical realities of motherhood, where the woman offers her body as home for the precious child (Stein 1956). I would add that in this era, when abortion is available, legal and socially accepted, childbirth is no longer assumed to be the inevitable result of sexual intercourse. The choice for motherhood, therefore, requires more conscious attention to the special value of the child.

In a Different Voice by Carol Gilligan (1982) introduces an idea I found new and illuminating. It is thought that girls become more empathetic because their mothers identify with them as females, whereas boys seem different to the mother. On the other hand, Simone de Beauvoir claims in *The Second Sex* that because women did not used to compete with men at work, they ratified rather than rivaled the men in their lives. A woman gives a man a kind of rebirth through her faith in him.

The nurturing function of woman can also be related to her special manner of using her mind. Housewifery, according to Simone de Beauvoir, means giving attention to little things in a limited sphere. While de Beauvoir insists that such a life is an intolerable restriction, G. K. Chesterton, in *What's Wrong with the World?* (1942, 153ff.), argues that work in the home is gloriously universalist and superior to the specialized tasks of masculine work in the world. The wife and mother is simultaneously sage, psychologist, doctor, cook, manager, teacher etc. Writing at the time of early English feminism, he found it contradictory that women wanted to rush out of their homes to do for strangers what they could do more successfully for their own dear families. He quipped that in his time thousands of women shouted, "We will not be dictated to any more", then rushed out with their stenopads to take dictation!

An idea of Karl Stern, which I have substantiated by observation, concerns the motives of a woman's thinking process. When men express their ideas, they concentrate on concepts, moving from concept to concrete examples and then returning to the concept. A woman is concerned about the listener's needs; she hunts for a truth that will be relevant to her listener and explains her thoughts in terms of that truth. It would be interesting to study women teachers to test my assumption that they frequently use personal examples, not only for the sake of clarity, but also to make ideas directly significant to the lives of their pupils.

In a novel about women intellectuals (*Gaudy Night*, 1936), Dorothy Sayers explores the idea that although women can be just as brilliant artists or thinkers as men can, there are few women who believe that such creativity is equal to the creativity of love and motherhood.

The concept that women are nurturers is not amorphous. It permeates our culture in vivid images of feminine heroines. I find a strong contrast, for example, between the characters Melanie and Scarlett, from the famous movie *Gone with the Wind*. Melanie represents all the sweet goodness of positive femininity. Scarlett, in selfish pursuit of her own goals, tramples on the needs of those to whom she should be most sensitive. In a climactic scene, she throws herself down a long flight of stairs rather than go through motherhood a second time.

The great Russian novel *Anna Karenina* also depicts a nurturing woman, Katya, whose virtues are highlighted by the portrayal of an opposite type of woman, Anna. Anna's desire for personal romantic fulfillment leads her inexorably to abandon not only her undeserving negative-masculine husband but finally her beloved son. Obsessed by jealousy of her lover, she can get little joy from the birth of their "love child" and refuses to attempt to conceive the son her lover longs for. In Tolstoy's tragic story, Katya, who chose real love after being rejected in her infatuation-love, enjoys the contentment of motherhood. Anna, who plunged into the world of eros and desperately sought life, ends in suicide, the total negation of life.

Mary, the Mother of God and the archetypal woman, enters our culture not only spiritually but also visually through millions of paintings and statues. She is depicted as full of compassion and tenderness for the infant Jesus and for us, her spiritual children.

Many of the active women saints are women of universal love, who reach out to help the poor and needy and long to comfort them with their own hands, their own tenderness.

In my childhood on Mother's Day it was traditional to hear a sugary sentimental song on the radio called "Mother", in which each letter of the word stood for some maternal virtue. Magazine and TV advertisements induced people to buy their food products by showing a warm, round, motherly type of woman preparing or serving the product.

On the opposite side, women who lacked nurturing qualities have always been excoriated in fairy tales, literature and the movies. The evil stepmother of Hansel and Gretel, the bad queen in Snow White, the cruel mother of Cinderella—these women must come to a bad end. So, too, do cold, self-absorbed women like Ibsen's Hedda Gabbler. Films in the 40s and 50s monotonously opened with plucky, aggressive women who, by the end of the movie, had been conquered and "feminized" by persistent men.

Most women accepted such images, not because they were weak and silly, but because some deep, earthy wisdom told them that the nurturing qualities of women were essential, and there could be no substitute for them.

In case you are getting nervous at this point, let me remind you that my title includes feminine and free. By the end of the book I hope to have shown that a woman's strength, vitality and sense of adventure need not be sacrificed to be feminine, but they can be part of it.

Let us turn now, however, to the negative distortions of nurturing that were outlined earlier: nagging, possessiveness and smothering.

Some time ago, I witnessed a scene in New York City that has helped me to understand how these distortions come about. A tiny, filthy playground, which had been built among the tall buildings, had no heavy rubber safety pads under the equipment. Tiny tots would climb up a huge slide and, if their mothers didn't catch them at the bottom, would land with a thud on the concrete. I shall never forget the touching sight of toddlers gleefully screeching their way down the slide, while their mamas stood tensely, arms outstretched, faces taut, waiting to rescue them from brain concussions.

This scene became a prime example to me of what philosophers call "contingency". Being finite, fragile human beings, we can be killed instantly by the slightest accident. We are contingent beings, not an absolute being like God, who remains solidly perfect no matter what happens. The fact of contingency poses a difficult and sometimes unbearable problem for those who love others. When we so keenly appreciate the preciousness of another individual—a child, a husband, a parent, a friend—how can we not become worried, and even paralyzed with fear, at the thought of all the dangers that threaten the beloved?

The child sees the world as a wonderful place of possibility, while the mother may come to view it as pure danger. Nagging can be analyzed as a petty way of trying to insure that things go well for loved ones. "Brush your teeth", "comb your hair", "put on your rubbers", etc. All these orders are given to help prevent future suffering such as rotting teeth, social ostracism or a cold. Though not as extreme as possessiveness and smothering, nagging or henpecking can become extremely disagreeable to the victim. It is inimical to a free, fun-loving atmosphere.

In possessive smothering, the woman wraps herself like a cocoon around her loved ones. First she holds them safe against the frightening world. Then she tries to mold them into the image that she cherishes for them. Finally, control replaces any respect for their own individuality and freedom.

In a perceptive passage, the philosopher Edith Stein describes the negative traits of some women as "an unmeasured interest in other people . . . curiosity, and gossip coming from too much desire to penetrate into the life of others . . . *not tolerating silent growth"* (Stein 1956, 162, italics added). This eventuates in treating others as if they belonged to one—as one's own *thing*.

A woman might overcome such possessiveness by adopting a philosophical attitude, shrugging her shoulders and uttering a cliche phrase: "So what can I do about it?" or "What's the use of worrying?" Personally, I find that only a profound faith in God permits me to accept the myriad possibilities of suffering that threaten those I love. Only by putting them into God's hands can I release them from my own.

I have a few more ideas about possessiveness to present before turning to other topics.

A brilliant young student of mine, afflicted with a smothering parent, phrased it this way: "Bitchiness is fear screaming—this incinerates a man."

Simone de Beauvoir describes the woman who over-mothers this way: "her dream is contradictory—she would like her son to have unlimited power, yet held in the palm of her hand, dominating the world, yet on his knees before her. She keeps him homebound so that she can control him but also hates him for not being a champion" (de Beauvoir 1952, 487–88). Such a paradox can be described metaphysically in this way: a woman tries to put the boy or man back into her womb for fear he will transcend her, tries to close the gap by keeping him in.

M. Esther Harding (1971) devotes a fascinating, if troubling, chapter of her book *Woman's Mysteries* to "The Sacrifice of the Son". It is socially acceptable to a point, but psychologically dangerous, when a mother sacrifices all her own interests in total devotion to her child. When she behaves in this way, she overprotects the son, who later becomes unable to meet the harsh realities of the world. The son gains the power to become strong only when she pushes him out into the world.

I recall, with tender pride, an early episode in my relationship with my son. Full of admiration for the Montessori method of schooling young children, I sent my boy a little prematurely to such a nursery. I didn't realize that in this particular institution the smallest children would mingle with sixth graders in the playground during the long, undersupervised recesses. During his first week of nursery school, my two and a half year old child was clearly terrified of making his way among the ten year old giants. But the teacher told me not to worry, he would get used to it sooner or later. So, the third day, I drove him to the school and stood behind the wire fence. My heart breaking, I watched him slowly try to steer a path through the big boys to the safety of his teacher, who was across the yard. About three feet away he turned around and yelled to me, "Mommy, go away. Can't you see I can never do it with you standing there!"

The Black poet Audre Lorde wrote in a similar vein "boys whisper to their mothers 'Let us sleep in your bed' . . . but she closes the door. They become men" (Lorde 1978, 8).

Here we end our references to the psychological and sociological factors of nurturing. These readings strengthened me as a mother and helped me to understand how the idea of nurturing has been distorted.

I will now turn to similar considerations about charm.

Years ago teenage girls used to be sent to "charm school", in the hope that they would be transformed from gangling adolescents into suave young ladies. The very idea would make knowing adults smile, for we were sure that charm was a quality much too elusive to be taught. Of course, the graduates of charm school knew how to dress well, how to sit in company with demurely crossed legs rather than sprawled out all over a sofa, how to apply makeup discreetly but effectively, etc. But is this really the same as being charming? In the popular film *Gigi*, often shown on TV, a charming but ill-bred girl is tutored in sophistication in preparation for marriage to a rich man-about-town. It succeeds and he is horrified by the result.

Even when we analyze charm and identify its components—sweetness, expressiveness, receptivity and sensual openness—it remains somewhat elusive. Some women have all these qualities, yet somehow lack a certain piquant element that turns a pleasant, comfortable woman into a charming, feminine one.

Charm in women may well reflect how a father relates to his daughter. Psychologists recognize a certain stage of coquettishness in little girls. A father, brother or other male figure can respond to such flirtatiousness with delight or sometimes, afraid of responding with too much sensuality, with rejection or disgust. A mother may model charm for her daughter; although sometimes the more attractive a mother, the more inferior a daughter will feel, particularly if she is physically less beautiful. On the other hand, a puritanical mother may punish her daughter for being charming, label her as a manipulator of men or openly reject her as a potentially "bad" girl.

A negative response to wild, free, girlish traits can stifle natural charm, which I believe to be innate in all people, producing stiff, prudish, repressed and shy daughters. Quietness, when it is not caused by fear of rejection, can of course be a lovely ingredient in a charming woman.

The celibate woman is not prudish; rather she is wide open to the mystical love of God, which encompasses body as well as spirit. The puritanical virgin hates the body and cannot bear the idea of another person entering her. Authentic virginal purity can, nonetheless, be a strong positive ingredient in feminine loveliness as well as a Christian virtue.

Simone de Beauvoir claims that a man is attracted to a virgin because he thinks that if no one has used her she can belong to him completely. More cynically, Bertrand Russell in *Marriage and Morals* (excerpted in Mahowald 1978) predicted that without sociological reinforcement of purity, men would refuse to acknowledge as their own the children they had conceived with women who had many lovers. Hence the state would become the father of the children of the future!

A charming but pure woman can use the force of the erotic in the service of genuine love. She can learn how to bring delight into the lives of those around her without luring others into an ultimately unfulfilling intimacy.

Naturally, charm in all its facets plays a large role in relationships that have the promise of commitment. Some Christian writers, eager to keep young people from sin, exalt an ideal of brotherly and sisterly affection even for engaged couples. This, I believe, goes too far. It can lead to a lack of sensual openness later in the marriage because partners have come to view one another only in practical or purely spiritual terms. It sometimes results in postponed romantic relationships with partners other than the too-brotherly husband. A certain light flirtatiousness in courtship seems to be a positive feminine experience, even though it can become negative if expressed promiscuously.

Before describing some of the negative traits associated with feminine charm, I want to highlight the quality of sweetness so much revered in the past, and now in danger of extinction.

A charming woman, even if she is a free spirit with plenty of passion, is, at the same time, sweet. A more peaceful, contented woman may be "pink lacy" sweet, but there are red-hot ways of being sweet as well. Ice cream is sweet, but so is liqueur.

Sweetness can come in many different ways. It can be an expression of innocence, a feeling of surrender or a quality of compassion. Sweetness comes when its opposite, bitterness, either has never been allowed to develop or has been overcome.

The lack of sweetness can signify an unwillingness to be close to others, a desire to be barricaded behind a wall and to be hard and self-enclosed. Lack of sweetness can also come from immersion in practical tasks and a failure to develop the subtle nuances of love. The sarcastic woman directs her attention to everything ridiculous and defective in others. In contrast, the sweet woman sees the vulnerability behind the bad, and seeks to bring out the better side of others through her faith in them. Nietzsche's dictum, though itself somewhat sarcastic, pronounces a truth, "Woman learns how to hate in proportion as she forgets how to charm."

Such are some of the positive aspects of the feminine virtue of charm. But the word "charm" itself has an ambiguous flavor; we also think of magic charms and, with that, a feeling of danger arises.

In Chinese thought, the feminine "Yin" is dark, shady, stealthy, destructive and catlike. Love is full of the power to destroy, wrote Sappho, the Greek poetess of the seventh century B.C. Men are afraid of falling under the power of woman as in the famous biblical story of Samson and Delilah or in Shakespeare's *Antony and Cleopatra*.

The seductress uses her sensual openness, her apparent sweetness and empathy, to control men for her own ends. She recognizes in herself and in the man the irrational weakness that sensual love creates: "Love, the limb-loosener, the bitter-sweet torment, the wild beast there is no withstanding" (Sappho).

Gertrud von Le Fort, in *The Eternal Woman* (1962), insightfully notes that while the whore serves the male as his object, she both triumphs over him and watches him become a prey to the dark forces of life. In seduction, according to de Beauvoir, the woman drags the man out of his transcendent world of meaningful goals into her own irrational immanence. I wonder what a prostitute might say about such a sophisticated theory.

To focus on less extreme negative aspects of charm, we might view the coy, flattering woman as one who wants to please too much. Lacking a sense of her own strengths, she becomes gushy and sentimental in her desire to find good in others on whom she might rely.

The eighteenth-century philosopher Mary Wollstonecraft pointed out in *A Vindication of the Rights of Women* (excerpted in Mahowald, 1978) that if a woman cultivates only her charms and not her mind and spirit, she has no inner faculties to rely on in marriage, once the first period of delight is over. When a husband is bored with her superficial traits, she becomes coquettish with other men or vainly obsessed with her looks and clothing.

Wollstonecraft's point is relevant to the image of women presented in contemporary advertisements. The more shrunken the mind and spirit of a woman, the more she must add to her mask of physical perfection. Behind such foolishness lies a desperate plea—"Love me because I am so charming, so perfectly beautiful"— because there is no hope of being loved for more substantial qualities. Such a woman spends hours before the mirror working on her looks. Narcissism becomes a substitute for the missing self-love that would produce true feminine charm.

Sometimes a woman who devotes no time at all to her personal vanity puts enormous energy into creating a "charming home". Paradoxically, if her only aim is to present an image of perfection, people will not want to visit and her family will be miserable; it is only when a home's decoration is permeated with a love of beauty and a concern for the needs of the inhabitants that a house becomes a place people want to visit and live in.

Do we not find, once again, in our discussion of the psychological and sociological aspects of femininity that it is love that makes the difference between the negative and positive ways of being charming?

COMPLEMENTARITY

Philosophical thinking about the feminine is rarely considered without the masculine. Throughout history and across cultures many philosophers have pronounced some form of complementarity. Generally they agree that there are *intrinsic* physical, emotional and intellectual differences between men and women and that these differences make men and women complementary pairs.

Here are some of the complementary qualities of

the masculine and feminine that philosophers have distinguished:

Masculine	Feminine
objective	intuitive
analytic	wise
leader	follower
interest in wider world	domestic
task oriented	quality-of-life oriented
light	dark
good	evil
providing	nurturing
hard	soft, delicate
dominating, governing	subservient
brutal	sweet
strong of body and will	weak of body and will
head dominates	heart dominates
creating outside of self	creating within the womb
spiritually active	spiritually contemplative
future oriented	present oriented
sublime	beautiful
adult	childlike

Some philosophers think of men and women as different but equal in their fundamental dignity. These would include: Augustine, Thomas Aquinas, Rousseau, Kant, C. S. Lewis, the von Hildebrands, Edith Stein, Karl Stern, Stephen Clark, Karol Wojtyla and C. G. Allen. Other philosophers consider the differences to indicate basic inferiority of women. These would include: Pythagorean thinkers, Aristotle, Schopenhauer, Nietzsche and

Sartre (in part). Philosophers who emphasize the similarity between men and women are mentioned in the chapter "Freedom".

In my research on philosophers' views about the feminine and masculine, I have primarily used two sources: Mahowald's *Philosophy of Woman* (1978), which includes excerpts of many works, and *The Great Books* (Index). Some excerpts do indicate extreme ideas about inferiority of women. However, in some cases, to label a philosopher antiwoman on the basis of particular quotations can be misleading, especially in the case of Thomas Aquinas.

A distinction should also be made between complementarity of qualities and complementarity of roles. Quality-complementarians such as Dietrich von Hildebrand, Stern and Wojtyla (John Paul II), are primarily concerned that different traits of men and women be reinforced, whatever roles they play in life. Of course, roles of motherhood and fatherhood involve different qualities, but one does not find in quality-complementarity the same emphasis on men and women having opposite positions and tasks in society.

Here are a few typical theories of a quality-complementarian.

Edith Stein, a German phenomenologist who became a Carmelite nun, writes:

> I am convinced that the human species develops as a double species of "man" and "woman", that the human essence in which no traits should be missing shows a twofold development and that this whole structure has this specific character. There is a difference, not only of bodily structure and of certain physiological functions, but the whole somatic life is different, as well as the relation of the psyche and body. . . . The female species is characterized by the unity and wholeness of the entire

psycho-somatic personality and by the harmonious development of the faculties; the male species by the perfecting
of individual capacities to obtain record achievements. . . .

[Woman's] strength is the intuitive grasp of the
living concrete, especially of the personal element. She
has the special gift of making herself at home in the inner
world of others (Stein 1956, 142).

This gift is related intricately to woman's ability
to carry a child within her womb and to breast-feed.
Whether biologically a mother or not, her whole psyche
is geared toward holding others close. Men and women
have different rhythms of being.

It is in the philosophy of Dietrich von Hildebrand, as
summarized in *Man and Woman*, that we find a theory
that is specifically quality-complementarian, with little
concern about implications for role-complementarity.
This may be partly explained by the fact that von
Hildebrand was himself the youngest in a family of re-
markably creative and intelligent women. He surrounded
himself with the same kind of women throughout his
life—his second wife, Alice von Hildebrand, being a
philosopher and coauthor of several of his books.

Von Hildebrand thinks that men and women are equal
in nature and in their call to holiness, yet they are two
different *expressions* of human nature.

The difference in the personality structure of man and
woman remains an undeniable reality. If we try to delineate
these specifically feminine and masculine features, we
find in women a unity of personality by the fact that
heart, intellect and temperament are much more inter-
woven; whereas in man there is a specific capacity to
emancipate himself with his intellect from the affective
sphere (Dietrich von Hildebrand 1965, 13).

Alice von Hildebrand points out that the united personality of a woman makes isolated (promiscuous) sexual experiences more destructive for her than for a man. The man committing the same sins is equally culpable, but less annihilated, since he can more readily make sex simply a compartment of his life. In woman the personality is more in the foreground, in man his activities.

According to Dietrich von Hildebrand because men and women are complementary, they are spiritually ordered to each other and created for each other. Greater love is possible between them than between members of the same sex. There is more fruitfulness because of a certain tension between them, because of their delight in one another. They are more suited to meet in an I–thou communion than two of the same sex who join together to appreciate a reality outside themselves.

Perceptively, von Hildebrand saw that the positive masculine liberates woman from the negative feminine and that the positive feminine helps to bring men out of the negative masculine. In his view, men become less coarse, dried out and depersonalized when women are present and women become less petty, self-centered and hypersensitive in the presence of men. A man with a strong mind can lift women out of the sort of complacency they may fall into. A woman brings out a man's tenderness and responsibility.

Quality-complementarity with a modified role-complementarity is commanding attention from another source: the philosophical and papal writings of John Paul II. Before becoming Pope, in his beautiful book *Love and Responsibility*, Bishop Karol Wojtyla underscores the equal ontological dignity of women and men. "A woman is only capable of making herself a gift if she believes in her value as a person and in the value of the man to whom she gives herself—which he cannot be unless he affirms the value of her person!" (Wojtyla 1981, 129).

Yet, at the same time, he frequently alludes to complementary differences in feminine and masculine traits similar to the ones we have outlined earlier in this chapter, many of which have been influences in his own thinking.[1]

A playwright as well as a philosopher-theologian, John Paul II frequently captures in a phrase his perception of complementarity, as in: "A woman wants to be loved so that she can show love; a man wants to love so that he can be loved." Or, "Above all, the woman feels her role in marriage is to give herself. The man's experience is different: its psychological correlative is possession" (Wojtyla 1981, 89).

Familiaris Consortio, Pope John Paul II's Apostolic Exhortation on the Family (1981), crystallizes his ideas about men and women in the married state in more concrete terms. The most often quoted passage states that wives and mothers must not be *compelled* to work outside the home. In his Encyclical on work, *Laborem Exercens*, the Pope suggested a revolutionary plan that would have societies provide women with supplementary incomes so that they might comfortably remain in the home to tend their children without economic pressure to work outside the house.

While Pope John Paul II's ideas are primarily quality-complementarian, expressions of role-complementarity can be found in varying extents in the works of such philosophers as Aristotle, Augustine, Thomas Aquinas, Rousseau, Kant, Nietzsche and Stephen Clark. They

---

[1] Wojtyla (1981) see 110, 117, 125 ff., 17ff., 189.

believe that the stability and happiness of mankind is furthered by strong role differentiation, especially concerning males in leadership. The most consistent and thoroughly developed of these positions is Stephen Clark's. Since his concepts are based on Scripture, Saint Augustine and Thomas Aquinas, I will summarize these philosophies in the next section of this chapter, "The Feminine Transfigured in Christ".

Among the most striking and popular recommendations of role-complementarity we find such best-selling books as *The Total Woman* (Marabel Morgan, 1975). These books differ from the sober rendition of scholars and philosophers not only in their rollicking "how to" style, but also in their emphasis on the negative feminine traits. The most mocked image from a book by Helen Audelin (1980), *Fascinating Womanhood*, depicts a woman, who, eager to hold onto her husband, attempts to distract him from the lure of other women by greeting him at the door, scantily clad with cocktails in hand. According to these women authors, the more dependent, manipulative, weak, coy and kittenish the woman, the more she will draw out the positive masculine traits in her spouse.

The happy "success stories" that fill such books raise certain questions about how apt the label "negative" might be in our list of feminine traits. Can it be that some of these qualities, while toxic to society in general, can become positive within the marital union?

Deborah Grumbine—wife, mother of five and Catholic writer—thinks so. In *How to Be Happy and Holy in Your Own Home*, she writes about joy in sex and contentment in family relations, and she depicts a certain merry coyness and frank desirousness as the rewards a tired husband and wife deserve after a hard day of work. Grumbine also believes strongly in the subordination of wives to their husbands. This submissiveness is not passivity, however, for the wife should battle vehemently for whatever she thinks is right. However, when the husband and wife disagree, the husband has to break the tie not only to avoid chaos or divorce, but also to realize his responsible, forceful leadership qualities. A man in this position will rejoice to know that his decisions have brought happiness to his wife and children. Grumbine's book includes invaluable practical suggestions about happiness in marriage and family and I highly recommend it to all women.

It is my conviction that quality-complementarity contains precious truths and that role-complementarity, while sometimes too rigid, is basically helpful to women and men. The feminist critique of these theories will be evaluated in the following chapter, "Freedom".

Basically, I find that women who concentrate on developing masculine traits and on fulfilling masculine roles seem incomplete and unhappy. Women who develop their femininity yet also develop the traditionally masculine traits (such as those listed at the beginning of this section entitled "Complementarity") seem more fulfilled.

Yet, we are called to exemplify all the virtues, not just the feminine ones. Sometimes romanticism of the feminine or a strict definition of roles can lead to the sort of clinging violet, passive, lovable but weak woman, such as Edith Bunker of "All in the Family".

I find this deformation exhibited by some Catholic women who stay in canonically invalid marriages or continue living in a situation where they are physically or psychologically battered; they do not stay out of love but because they fear independence and the resulting struggle to earn a living. A less drastic form of inadequate development of traditionally more masculine traits occurs when a woman is too shy to witness her faith.

It is certainly true that men who overemphasize their male-leadership traits without developing Christian maturity can become, at worst, tyrannical and brutal, and, at best, patronizing, paternalistic and smug.

I have found it stimulating to consider an analysis of the feminine from the standpoint of natural knowledge and wisdom. However, for me this is but a prelude to the enjoyment of the truth to be found through pondering God's will for women in Scripture and tradition—the subject of the next portion of this chapter on femininity.

THE FEMININE TRANSFIGURED IN CHRIST

"In him all things were made" (Jn 1:3).

If I were raising a girl today, when the feminine is under attack, I would tell her from earliest childhood that God had planned her to be a female. "Male and female he created them" (Gen 1:27).

Just as Jesus said, God could count every hair on her head. He who "knit her together in her mother's womb" (Ps 139:13) certainly formed her as a unique personality to be manifest in the feminine form, in a female body.

Whenever my little daughter would see a cute baby I would tell her that some day she might be a mother and that this would be a great gift from God.

When I would read to her about the women saints who were sisters and nuns, I would explain that they had sacrificed being wives and mothers in order to be brides of Christ and that this made them not unsexed, but spiritual mothers.

I would also tell her about the holy single women who expressed their motherly warmth and care in tending the needy and in performing corporal and spiritual works of mercy. Their feminine charm was not stifled; it blossomed because of their love for Christ.

When my daughter began menstruating I would read to her about the martyrs and the stigmatists. She would learn that her own minor, but nonetheless perhaps painful, monthly bleeding was not only a way to participate in Christ's suffering on the Cross but also a way to prepare for her motherhood in the Kingdom. I would witness to her how I offered up my own monthly pain and discomfort for others, for the Kingdom.

When she began to show interest in boys, I would make explicit for her the meaning of sexual attraction and marriage.

> It is not good that the man should be alone; I will make him a helper fit for him. . . . So the Lord God caused a deep sleep to fall upon the man, and while he slept took one of his ribs and closed up its place with flesh; and the rib which the Lord God had taken from the man he made into a woman and brought her to the man. Then the man said, "This at last is bone of my bones and flesh of my flesh; she shall be called Woman, because she was taken out of Man." Therefore, a man leaves his father and his mother and cleaves to his wife, and they become one flesh (Gen 2:18–24).

Using examples from the love expressed daily in my own marriage, I would show her how the grace of this sacrament overcomes the dissension and hurt. I would explain why marriage is sacred and how Jesus reaffirmed this bond.

> And Pharisees came up to him and tested him by asking, "Is it lawful to divorce one's wife for any cause?" He answered, "Have you not read that he who made them from the beginning made them male and female, and said 'For this reason a man shall leave his father and mother and be joined to his wife, and the two shall become one'? . . . What therefore God has joined together let no man put asunder. . . . For your hardness of heart Moses allowed you to divorce your wives, but from the beginning it was not so" (Mt 19:3–9).

I would summarize for her, or let her read for herself when she was old enough, what John Paul II wrote in his book *Original Unity of Man and Woman* (1981) about the mystery of the attraction of man and woman for each other and the great difference between real love and lust (John Paul II 1981). I would have her read Dietrich von Hildebrand's beautiful book *Marriage* (1984).

I would explain to her about her own fertility and the sacredness of her time of creative openness and how evil it is to damage and pervert this sacred time by using contraceptives. I would use this analogy: sex is for love and reproduction, just as the church building is for prayer and for the Mass. It would be terrible if during the Consecration the priest brought together the bread and the wine and then proclaimed: "This is *not* my Body, *not* my Blood." So, too, how irreverent to bring together the sperm and the egg and yet introduce life-destructive elements between them to bring death instead of life.[2]

---

[2] For further discussion of Catholic teaching on this and other issues, see my book *Christian Ethics and Your Everyday Life* (1979); it provides texts from Scripture and tradition for many controversial issues.

Those convinced that for *serious* reasons they must postpone having a child can still use the nonfertile time to express their love.

If my daughter saw casual sex on TV or among her friends, I would tell her how it would violate her own feminine desire for real closeness and warmth to be seriously close to someone who does not cherish her enough to want her forever. I would point out to her that many engaged couples break up, showing their love was not meant for their whole lives as Christ wished true love to be.

I would use such intrinsic arguments as a foundation for the practical ones about not wanting to become pregnant when there is no "nest" for the baby. How sad that the child who will look like the beloved should be dreaded rather than cherished. What a demonic rebellion against God to try to undo nature as he made it by aborting a child in the womb!

I would teach her to use her intuitive gifts to distinguish between attraction that comes from loneliness and the real self-donation of a marriage in Christ.

When friends of mine were considering divorce I would explain to my daughter how tragic this was. In discussing cases in which the woman was primarily the victim or the marriage was invalid, I would counsel my daughter not to lose courage, but to see why that woman had been blessed: she had loved a man deeply and perhaps borne children who could never have been exactly those individuals except for that particular union of genes.

I would teach her to admire those brave unwed mothers who bear their children after repenting of a love affair and to pray for women who aborted their babies, that they find forgiveness in Christ.

I would urge her to remain at home with her children when they are young, and later to engage in part-time work outside the home if a supplementary income is needed or to develop her God-given talents that are not used in mothering.

If my daughter objected that since Vatican II many Catholics make up their own minds in conscience about ethical issues concerning their womanhood, I would provide direct quotations such as the following from the Documents of Vatican II:

> Often he [man] sets himself up as the absolute measure of all things. . . . Enlightened by divine revelation she [the Church] can offer a solution" (Flannery 1975, 913, *The Church in the Modern World*, 12).

> Deep within his conscience, man discovers a law which he has not laid upon himself but which he must obey. Its voice, ever calling him to love and to do what is good and to avoid evil, tells him inwardly at the right moment: do this, shun that. For man has in his heart a law inscribed by God. His dignity lies in observing this law, and by it he will be judged. His conscience is man's most secret core, and his sanctuary. There he is alone with God whose voice echoes in his depths. By his conscience, in a wonderful way, that law is made known which is fulfilled in the love of God and of one's neighbor. Through loyalty to conscience, Christians are joined to other men in the search for truth and for the right solution to so many moral problems which arise both in the life of individuals and from social relationships. Hence, the more correct conscience prevails, the more do persons and groups turn aside from blind choice, and try to be guided by the objectivity standards of moral conduct (Flannery 1975, 916, *The Church in the Modern World*, 16).

Today there is an inescapable duty to make ourselves the neighbor of every man, no matter who he is and, if we meet him, to come to his aid in a positive way, whether he is an aged person abandoned by all, a foreign worker despised without reason, a refugee, an illegitimate child wrongly suffering for a sin he did not commit, or a starving human being who awakens our conscience by calling to mind the words of Christ: "As you did it to one of the least of these my brethren, you did it to me" (Mt 25:40).

The varieties of crime are numerous: all offenses against life itself, such as murder, genocide, abortion, euthanasia and willful suicide; all violations of the integrity of the human person, such as mutilation, physical and mental torture, undue psychological pressures; all offenses against human dignity, such as subhuman living conditions, arbitrary imprisonment, deportation, slavery, prostitution, the selling of women and children, degrading working conditions where men are treated as mere tools for profit rather than free and responsible persons: all these and the like are criminal; they poison civilization; and they debase the perpetrators more than the victims and militate against the honor of the creator (Flannery 1975, 928, *The Church in the Modern World*, 27).

The well-being of the individual person and of both human and Christian society is closely bound up with the healthy state of conjugal and family life. Hence Christians today are overjoyed, and so too are all who esteem conjugal and family life highly, to witness the various ways in which progress is being made in fostering those partnerships of love and in encouraging reverence for human life; there is progress too in services available to married people and parents for fulfilling their lofty calling: even greater benefits are to be expected and efforts are being made to bring them about.

However, this happy picture of the dignity of these partnerships is not reflected everywhere, but is overshadowed by polygamy, the plague of divorce, so-called free love, and similar blemishes; furthermore, married love is too often dishonored by selfishness, hedonism, and unlawful contraceptive practices. Besides, the economic, social, psychological, and civil climate of today has a severely disturbing effect on family life. . . .

The intimate partnership of life and love which constitutes the married state has been established by the creator and endowed by him with its own proper laws: it is rooted in the contract of its partners, that is, in their irrevocable personal consent. It is an institution confirmed by the divine law and receiving its stability, even in the eyes of society, from the human act by which the partners mutually surrender themselves to each other; for the good of the partners, of the children, and of society this sacred bond no longer depends on human decision alone. For God himself is the author of marriage and has endowed it with various benefits and with various ends in view: All of these have a very important bearing on the continuation of the human race, on the personal development and eternal destiny of every member of the family, on the dignity, stability, peace, and prosperity of the family and of the whole human race. By its very nature the institution of marriage and married love is ordered to the procreation and education of the offspring and it is in them that it finds its crowning glory. Thus the man and woman, who "are no longer two but one" (Mt 19:6), help and serve each other by their marriage partnership; they become conscious of their unity and experience it more deeply from day to day. The intimate union of marriage, as a mutual giving of two persons, and the good of the children demand total fidelity from the spouses and require an unbreakable unity between them (Flannery 1975, 950, *The Church in the Modern World*, 47, 48).

God, the Lord of life, has entrusted to men the noble mission of safeguarding life, and men must carry it out in a manner worthy of themselves. Life must be protected with the utmost care from the moment of conception: abortion and infanticide are abominable crimes. Man's sexuality and the faculty of reproduction wondrously surpass the endowments of lower forms of life; therefore the acts proper to married life are to be ordered according to authentic human dignity and must be honored with the greatest reverence. When it is a question of harmonizing married love with the responsible transmission of life, it is not enough to take only the good intention and the evaluation of motives into account; the objective criteria must be used, criteria drawn from the nature of the human person and human action, criteria which respect the total meaning of mutual self-giving and human pro-creation in the context of true love; all this is possible only if the virtue of married chastity is seriously practiced. In questions of birth regulation the sons of the Church, faithful to these principles, are forbidden to use methods disapproved of by the teaching authority of the Church in its interpretation of the divine law.

Let all be convinced that human life and its transmission are realities whose meaning is not limited by the horizons of this life only: their true evaluation and full meaning can only be understood in reference to man's eternal destiny (Flannery 1975, 954–5, *The Church in the Modern World*, 51).

Women should also read *Familiaris Consortio*, The Apostolic Exhortation on the Family (1981), for beautifully articulated affirmations of Church teaching on the family and also on the witness of virgins. In this document, as elsewhere, Pope John Paul II raises important points about social ethics. The feminine role of maternity must be supported by society. Women who would wish to be full-time mothers must not be forced to work outside the home.

Certain feminist positions concerning maternity and paternity leave, flexible time for mothers and fathers, equitable laws concerning credit, etc., should be complemented, I believe, by greater parish involvement in support services for women at all phases of their lives.

Let us turn to another topic concerning the feminine transfigured in Christ. My hypothetical daughter might be quite troubled about marriage and wonder how to make decisions. Some of her Christian friends might believe in following literally the words of Saint Paul and Saint Peter in passages such as these:

> Be subject to one another out of reverence for Christ. Wives, be subject to your husbands, as to the Lord. For the husband is the head of the wife as Christ is the head of the Church, his body, and is himself its savior. As the Church is subject to Christ, so let wives also be subject in everything to their husbands. Husbands, love your wives, as Christ loved the Church and gave himself up for her, that he might sanctify her, having cleansed her by washing of water with the word. . . . Even so husbands should love their wives as their own bodies. He who loves his wife loves himself. . . . Let each of you love his wife as himself, and let the wife see that she respects her husband (Eph 5:21–33).

> Likewise, you wives, be submissive to your husbands, so that some, though they do not obey the word, may be won without a word by the behavior of their wives, when they see your reverent and chaste behavior. Let not

yours be the outward adorning with braiding of hair, decoration of gold, and wearing of robes, but let it be the hidden person of the heart with the imperishable jewel of a gentle and quiet spirit, which in God's sight is very precious. . . . Let nothing terrify you.

Likewise, you husbands, live considerately with your wives, bestowing honor on the woman as the weaker sex, since you are joint heirs of the grace of life, in order that your prayers may not be hindered. Finally, all of you, have unity of spirit, sympathy, love of the brethren, a tender heart and a humble mind. Do not return evil for evil or reviling for reviling; but on the contrary, bless, for to this you have been called, that you may obtain a blessing (1 Pet 3:1–9).

Here I would warn her about extremities in male headship, yet have her ponder the views of Saint Augustine, Saint Thomas Aquinas and of the contemporary writer Stephen Clark.

Saint Augustine, in the *Confessions* (Book IX), described his mother, Saint Monica, as subject to her husband through God. She spoke about God to her pagan husband as often as she could. For the sake of God she submitted to her husband's lust and anger. When he exploded in anger she would calm him down and then give her side of the matter. For her own sake, to avoid his constant anger, she played the role of servant. Finally, she succeeded in bringing her husband to Christ through her peaceful methods. After his conversion, his character was reformed. In other words, by taking submission to be a positive feminine trait she was able to help her husband abandon his negative masculine traits and assume positive ones. The Christian man does rule his obedient wife; Christian rule is a service of love in duty and must never come out of love of power.

Although he accepted different roles for men and women, Saint Augustine understood those passages which state that man and woman were made in the image of God as proof, beyond doubt, that women and men are equal in mind and soul (*Confessions*, Book XIII). Saint Thomas Aquinas followed Saint Augustine in this matter. He thought women were equal to men in spiritual dignity but had weaker wills and hence were in need of male leadership.

Stephen Clark (1980) presents one of the most thoroughly developed theories on male leadership, one that is based on Scripture.

These are the key premises of Clark's argument:

— There is a truth about how people ought to live that God communicates to us through Scripture and tradition; what we believe to be God's truth should be followed as authoritative and normative.

— Study of Scripture on this topic must begin as Jesus did by understanding God's intent in creating male and female as it is expressed in Genesis.

— Even if the Genesis texts are, in part, to be interpreted symbolically, this does not preclude the idea that the essentials are God given. "Male and female in the image of God" shows spiritual and metaphysical equality. "Out of the rib" means women are of the same species. "Flesh of flesh" means, not dependence, but covenant unity. Companionship in the Old Testament does not so much mean I–thou communication as it means helping each other to produce and raise the family. "Your husband shall rule over you" *does not mean domination or inferiority* but rather subordination: one person is ordered under the direction of another for the sake of unity. Man represents the family as its leader within the wider community; he sets the direction of the family, protects it and provides for it.

— To be subordinate *does not connote inferiority*, except to those who fail to see that obedience to legitimate authority is a virtue. Jesus obeys Mary and Joseph but is not inferior to them. A son obeys a father without being inferior in nature. The Son obeys the Father without being inferior. The Church has a hierarchy of authority without connoting any inferiority in dignity.

The word "subordinate" is ambiguous. Types of subordination include:

a. Domination by coercion, force, slavery. Here oppression benefits the ruler at the expense of the ruled. This is not Christian subordination at all.

b. Mercenary—to bargain for money. May be voluntary and is sometimes legitimate, for example in work situations.

c. Voluntarily willed for the sake of unity and care, as in the case of family, discipleship and community. It is based not on imposing one's own standards, but rather on ethical and religious norms. Male leadership entails this voluntary subordination.

In the next chapter, "Freedom", we will see why Stephen Clark regards the feminist revolution against male leadership to be fatal for harmonious family living.

In general, I would want to witness to my daughter that it is worthwhile to "lay down one's life" for others in imitation of Christ. I would hope she would see from my own example that one does not need to be perfect to be a wife and mother. Nor need one be perfect to be a single woman for Christ or to be a consecrated woman— for Christ is all-forgiving, eager to erase the past and to give us fresh energies to bear the burden of our womanly roles.

By being close to Christ in the sacraments and in prayer, we can fulfill our great feminine vocation: to live out our love for others day by day in faithfulness.

Finally, I would have my daughter steep herself in Marian devotion and frequently read the lives of women saints so that she could see how beautiful they were in their feminine warmth, charm and faithfulness.

A reader interested in pursuing this love for Mary and the saints might want to try a method I devised with Sister Mary Neill in our book *Bringing The Mother with You: Healing Meditations on the Mysteries of Mary* (1982) and in a forthcoming book by us on the saints.

Healing of the Feminine

Perhaps the hypothetical daughter I created in the previous section would not need healing prayer. Most of us, however, have been distorted to some extent, in our own appropriation of our feminine natures. At various workshops I have suggested some paths for healing that seem to be effective:

1. Ponder in prayer the question of why you were created by God to be a woman.

2. Read the following passages from Scripture and see if they speak to you personally about the virtues mentioned:

gentleness: Prov 15:4; Jer 11:19; Jn 8 (Christ's gentleness to the woman taken in adultery); Mt 5:22; Mt 11:29; Gal 5:22.

compassion: Dt 13:17; Ps 145:9; Is 40:1–2; Is 54:8; Is 66:12; Hos 11; Lk 7:13; Lk 10:29ff.; Lk 15; Lk 23:34; Col 3:12.

obedience: Ex 24:7; Is 1:19; Lk 2:15; Lk 4; Mt 26:39; Rom 6; 1 Pet 1:13–14; 2 Tim 4:1–5; 1 Pet 3:1–7; 1 Tim 2:9–15; 1 Cor 14:34; Eph 5:22–33; Titus 2:5.

purity: Ps 24:4; Ps 51; Mt 5:8; Mt 5:28; Gal 5:19; Rom 1:26; Jude 1:7; Titus 2:5, 12; 1 Pet 3:1–7.

3. Return to the list of feminine traits that opened this chapter. You might thank God for the positive ones you checked. Alone or with a prayer partner you might look at your negative feminine traits and try to find their roots, then pray for healing of them. You could also pray to receive the positive traits you identified as ones you wish you had.

4. If you seek further healing in this area you might want to listen to some tapes I have made, which are distributed by Dove (Pecos, New Mexico 87552).

Freedom

A woman wants not only to be feminine but also to be free.

Listed here are some traits that some people associate with freedom. Check the ones you think you have and circle the ones you wish you had (or make separate lists).

adventuresome	just
ambitious	leading
assertive	logical
authoritative	loud
brave	lustful
cold	objective
competitive	proud
daredevilish	ruthless
daring	self-controlled
decisive	spontaneous
domineering	strong
driving	stubborn
firm	tough
forceful	valiant
initiating	

Generally, in my experience, people would divide these qualities in terms of negative and positive this way:

Positive Traits of a Free Woman

adventuresome, assertive, authoritative, brave, daring, decisive, driving, firm, forceful, initiating, just, leading, logical, objective, self-controlled, spontaneous, strong, tough, valiant

Famous women who have exhibited some of these traits include: Esther, Deborah, Judith, Saint Catherine of Siena, Saint Teresa of Avila, Saint Joan of Arc, Harriet Tubman, Amelia Earhart, Eleanor Roosevelt, Rose Kennedy, Golda Meir. You can probably add many more.

Negative Traits of a Free Woman

ambitious, cold, competitive, daredevilish, domineering, loud, lustful, proud, ruthless, stubborn

Examples of women who have exhibited some of these negative traits include: Herodias, who ordered the beheading of John the Baptist; Livia, the scheming Roman dowager from the time of the Caesars; Lady Macbeth; Lucretia Borgia and Joan Crawford (if her daughter's account is true).

This chapter first discusses the concept of freedom and then focusses on certain key traits in this area:

spontaneity and daring versus repression or folly
strength to lead versus passivity or domineeringness
objectivity versus subjectivity or cold analysis

How a woman's positive freedom and strength support her feminine nature will be explained.

We will investigate the roots of freedom and consider two methods for gaining greater freedom for women: feminist assertiveness and Jungian wholeness.

A section of this chapter, "Freedom Transfigured in Faith", will show how the inspiration of the Holy Spirit is the source of true freedom together with obedience to the Spirit as he works through the Pope and the bishops in union with him. This section also considers problems connected with patriarchy, language and women's roles in the Church structure.

Finally, there will be suggestions for spiritual healing for greater freedom.

THE NATURE OF FREEDOM

Freedom can be defined in several ways: exemption or liberation from control by another person or by some arbitrary power; liberty; independence; ease of performance, openness, unrestrictedness.

Philosophers like to speak of the difference between "freedom from" and "freedom to". "Freedom from" implies absence of coercion. During World War II there was a popular German song "die Gedenken sind frei"; its theme was that no amount of external force could control one's thoughts.

Women naturally want to feel free from such extreme forms of enslavement as forced marriage, rape or battering. We would also like to be free from demeaning judgments that would keep us in unfulfilling roles.

Freedom to—or liberty—implies more. It involves the power to bring about what is good. This depends not only on the absence of coercion but also on the interior strength to be an instrument of the good and hence, too, on the freedom from enslavement to our own psychological complexes or vices.

In this sense women hope to develop their talents and

also their virtues to become promoters of improvement in conditions in the family, society and Church.

In the absence of a philosophy of human nature and clear-cut goals, freedom can become trivial or dangerous. In these cases it is called whimsy or license.

Let us look at some elements in the free personality to see how these can be integrated with the feminine.

We think of a woman as repressed or conformist if she is unable to act in a spontaneous and daring manner. We do not applaud a woman whose actions are foolhardy or silly, but we very much enjoy the company of a woman with flair.

Consider the contrast between the two main women characters of the popular movie, *The Sound of Music*. The sophisticated middle-aged woman who hopes to marry the hero is stiff and conformist. Maria is spontaneous, creative and daring. At first, these qualities of the younger woman frighten her rather unimaginative employer but gradually they delight and rejuvenate him.

It is easy to see that spontaneity is an ingredient of feminine charm. In fact, it helps prevent natural charm from congealing into studied manipulation.

To be a leader requires the freedom of real strength. The word "leader", as used here, should not be interpreted too narrowly. A queen or a prime minister is a leader but so is a mother of children. A writer or artist may be a leader but so is a teacher. Passive, weak, dependent women lack such freedom. Domineering women appear to be strong but really lack inner freedom. It is insecurity that motivates them to try to control every person and every situation they encounter.

The element of strength is important, if nurturing, warm, feminine qualities are to triumph over the fear that comes from weakness. How often in the tragic story of an abortion we find a nice, young woman, eager to be loving, who was too weak to avoid premarital sex, too frightened to seek the help of her parents, too weak to suffer the discomfort of being pregnant in order to give up the baby for adoption, and certainly too weak to fend for herself as a single parent. Strength of character would have complemented her warm disposition and helped her to say No to sex or, afterward, to make the sacrifices necessary to help, rather than destroy, her baby.

Another aspect of the free personality is objectivity. To use freedom to choose the good, one must know what is really beneficial in life. Objectivity is not synonymous with the negative, often masculine, traits of being cold, overly analytical and critical. These personality defects arise not so much from a love of truth but from the desire to dominate, perhaps because of an exaggerated fear of making mistakes, or in order to show superiority.

Without objectivity a woman's choices can often be unrealistically sentimental or easily influenced by others.

Men sometimes laugh at so-called women's intuition because it is not always checked by other means of arriving at truth. A fine example would be Lucy Ricardo in "I Love Lucy". Lucy is full of charm, but this positive feminine trait gets swamped in her silly lack of realism.

By contrast, the intuition of women strong in common sense and, even further, in contact with the deepest realities is rich and fruitful. A contrasting television character would be Olivia, the wife and mother of "The Waltons".

In this section we will concentrate on the question of strength versus weakness. Most women who want to achieve more freedom do so for the sake of greater power.

Often, we think of strength as a masculine trait. As shown in the chapter "Femininity", men on the average are biologically stronger in muscular power. In contrast, women have greater longevity and, of course, the physical potency for nurturing a baby in the womb and at the breast.

A woman can also be powerful within a culture in which matriarchal structures prevail or when circumstances make her the natural heir or property holder.

Psychologically some women become tough as they battle against "macho" men. Because they detest roles of enslavement or being bullied, some women develop their physical and emotional strength to a competitive level. Usually, such power is gained at the expense of feminine qualities of warmth and charm, but not always.

Because of the superior muscular strength of men and the subordinate roles women play in many cultures, most women try to win strength in order to triumph over feelings of weakness and vulnerability. A woman realizes that in this process she may have to sacrifice the security that comes from assuming secondary roles—the consequent approval and protection of men.

As is clear from the chapter on the feminine, it is not my contention that women should not play helping roles; however, women should come to these complementary endeavors with peaceful strength not servile dependency.

A ghastly case of dependency and vulnerability, which

played to a tragic last act, was the center of public attention in 1980. Jean Harris, a successful fifty-six-year-old career woman, presumably killed the man who had been her lover for fourteen years because of his affair with a younger woman. (She had tried first to kill herself.) In a fascinating article about the way American women passionately identified with Jean Harris, writer Erica Abeel pointed out the threat this story poses to the new feminists. Before this event, Jean Harris might have represented the new independent woman that many wish to become. Since she had accepted a lifestyle that was free from commitments—she chose a love affair over the stodgy realities of marriage—why was Jean Harris not strong enough to accept the consequences? "But in some bottom layer she [Jean Harris] wasn't the modern self-reliant woman she appeared. Later she would lack the resources, toughness and coolness essential to that role. Harris had the trappings of independence—but they overlaid dangerous residues from the past. Like the inability to make work the sustaining center it must be if you plan to go it alone. Like the tendency to place not work, but a man—*one* man at the center of your life" (Abeel 1981, 50).

Let us go a bit more systematically into the nature of vulnerability in its negative aspects, which are so opposite to true freedom.

One form of weakness found sometimes among North American women, but more frequently in some other cultures, is passivity. In the face of life's difficulties and seemingly inexorable suffering, a woman can adopt an attitude of false resignation—"peace" is achieved by expecting little and enduring all. The price to pay for male support is total submission.

Of course, such passivity may stimulate negative masculine traits of cruelty. In *No Exit* (1949), Jean-Paul Sartre's anti-hero, Garcin, describes how his wife's servile passivity disgusts him. He commits worse and worse sins against marital love in order to arouse her anger. Finally, he brings a whore right into their spousal bed and forces his wife to serve them breakfast the next morning.

To give up hope like this may seem slavish to women with independent natures, but the motive may not be to idolize the oppressor; it may instead be an attempt to find one's own equilibrium by refusing to react. In the increasing problem of wife beating, defined as "serious and repeated physical injury from deliberate assaults by the spouse", we can find passivity reinforced by social inequality (Hilberman 1980, 1337). In 1968 twenty percent of the population of the United States approved of wife beating, and forty percent of all female homicide victims were killed by their husbands. Women are afraid to leave their homes, not only because their spouses threaten reprisal, but also because they lack support for themselves and their children. Accustomed to defining themselves dependently, they cannot imagine fending for themselves in the outside world.

In religious women such fears can be hidden by a veneer of "martyrdom" in the name of bearing a cross for the Lord. True religious detachment is quite different from such passive resignation. Hopelessness is diametrically opposed to valiant hope in God.

In the middle and upper classes, another form of passivity can be found among parasitic women. Esther Vilar in *The Manipulated Man* (excerpted in Mahowald 1978) humorously describes the way in which many women avoid intellectual challenges in order to relax into the torpor of repetitive housewifely existence:

By the age of twelve at the latest, most women have decided to become prostitutes. Or, to put it another way, they have planned a future for themselves which consists of choosing a man and letting him do all the work. In return for his support, they are prepared to let him make use of their vagina at certain given moments. The minute a woman has made this decision she ceases to develop her mind . . . rarely using the time she has gained (by the inventions of men to lessen housework) for an active interest in history, politics, or astrophysics, the woman bakes cakes, irons underclothes, and makes ruffles and frills for blouses, or, if she is especially enterprising, covers her bathroom with flower decals.

Germaine Greer in *The Female Eunuch* draws a biting caricature of the stereotype of the fashion ads, a sterile unreal woman whose only concern is to create an image of glamour:

In that mysterious dimension where the body meets the soul, the stereotype is born and has her being. . . . To her belongs all that is beautiful . . . all that exists to beautify her. The sun shines only to burnish her skin and gild her hair; the wind blows only to whip up the color in her cheeks; the sea strives to bathe her; flowers die gladly so that her skin may luxuriate in their essence. . . . Baby seals are battered with staves, unborn lambs ripped from their mother's wombs, millions of moles, muskrats, squirrels, minks . . . and other small and lovely creatures die untimely deaths that she might have furs (Greer 1972, 51).

If passivity is incompletely achieved, a woman may find herself without the strength to act meaningfully in the world, but unable to resign herself to the sufferings that afflict her. Simone de Beauvoir (1952) writes that finding the world menacing, but outside of her control, a woman worries instead of acting. Since everything happens to her through the agency of others, she develops a psychology of complaint and rage. Sometimes, because she refuses to assume responsibility, she does not see the world in its complexity, but instead as pure good (herself and those closest to her) versus pure evil ("they").

"Hysteria" in the popular sense of the term, uncontrolled rage, can be a woman's way of constantly accusing those who dominate her. In this aggressive-passive behavior, a woman will make a tremendous fuss so that everyone around must share in her discomfort, yet she never actually does anything assertive to change her bad situation.

Negative feminine intellectual traits such as silliness and naiveté can also be related to passivity. Unwilling to take the trouble to study and analyze the world around her, a woman may instead adopt a set of oversimplistic cliches or childish excuses for ignorance. Sometimes very intelligent women lapse into silliness as a ruse to avoid losing masculine affection. It has been shown that many more women than men introduce ideas with "disclaimers", such as, "I really don't know much about this, but here is one idea, just my own opinion", instead of forthrightly proclaiming an idea with confidence. Much more active displays of weakness include clinging, obsession and idol worship.

Here is how negative intellectual traits can feed into these other negative emotional traits. A woman without a strong focus, according to Edith Stein (1956), tends to nibble in all directions seeking wholeness; she is unable to develop one gift thoroughly because she lacks confidence. Such an uncomfortable state of existence easily propels a woman toward anyone who appears to have direction or power. How thrilling to ride the tail of the comet. How meaningful to be part of the life of a man who is "going somewhere". Freud thought women lacked libido. Living vicariously off the life energies of another—be it a male, a stronger female or a child—can best be accomplished by the close proximity that comes with slavish devotion.

Negative feminine traits such as manipulativeness come into play here, as the woman seeks to secure the presence of her "idol". Simone de Beauvoir incisively points out that even if the man is asked to give nothing in return for the woman's undying affection, he is still being forced to give up his own freedom of movement in order to be present to receive the numerous material and emotional gifts the woman wants so much to indulge him with.

Resentment and spite often follow idol worship, once the clay feet become visible. The European psycho-therapist Ida Gorres says that to men, women seem like prowling time bombs. Tied to a particular man as his lover, wife, secretary or assistant, the disappointed woman seeks ways to vent her anger at his failure to live up to her dreams of his perfection. The love relationships of some male homosexuals, those of an effeminate nature, display similar patterns.

In extreme cases, a woman's sense of self becomes so deficient, through years of dependence, that she will decide to commit suicide if she is threatened with the loss of her worshipped male idol. Of course, there can be other reasons (such as abandonment in early childhood) why the loss of a love object can seem devastating. In any case, how tragic to throw away the whole world with all its beauty, goodness and promise for the love of one puny mortal! Rightly, a psychologist dealing with a patient, female or male, who wants to take his own life because of unrequited love, looks not at the cruelty of the rejecting party, but at the lack of self-esteem and the narrowness of emotional focus of the suicidal person.

Given such shipwreck, is it any wonder that people try to hide their vulnerability behind a mask of pseudo-strength?

There are two principal contemporary ideologies that seek to strengthen women in their battle against their own feelings of weakness: one is feminism, the other is wholeness theory. We will explore these philosophies and their practical applications, and we will cite relevant thinkers of the past. These two movements will also be evaluated for their positive and negative features.

FEMINISM

The word "feminism" is somewhat ambiguous. Linked to the phrase "women's liberation", it seems to signify the desire to defend the rights of women against various subtle and extreme forms of oppression.

At first, the woman's liberation movement of the late 60s and early 70s appeared simply to be the rejection of negative masculine exploitation of women in all its societal forms. It emphasized replacing the enslavement of roles determined by gender with the freedom to choose whatever one might want to do in life.

Gradually a distinction was made between moderate feminism and radical feminism. The latter insisted on more extreme measures to end oppression, such as the abolition of marriage and even of sexual relations with men.

Simultaneously there arose a different, if sympathetic, branch of feminism that emphasized the affirmation of feminine values and lobbied for social reform in consonance with those values. An analogy can be made here with the evolution of the Black Movement in America. At first, liberation meant gaining equal rights with the majority White population. Then a current which developed within the leadership emphasized "Black is beautiful." Their goal was not to become like "whitey" but instead to delight in what was different in Black appearance and culture.

So too, a branch of feminism has arisen that stresses that what is distinctly feminine is beautiful. With this idea came a desire to see society changed so that it fosters such womanly values as motherhood. Maternity leave, for instance, is an idea designed to support the special childbearing function of the female body, rather than view it as a liability.

However, the idea that women have dignity and rights was not invented by the women's liberation movement in the nineteenth century.

In the fifth century B.C. Plato wrote his dialogue the *Symposium*, which included his famous myth about the sexes. According to the myth, human beings used to be both male and female in the same entity. This then was our original whole state. But then they were cut in half into distinct male and female beings. Ever since they have sought longingly to find their missing halves. This accounts for the vehemence of the sex drive.

It is in Book V of the *Republic* that Plato developed his most revolutionary ideas about women. Equal in mind, women are to have equal educational opportunities and the same roles, including military service. He thought it desirable to devise a system of communal wives that included eugenic childbreeding and permitted promiscuity after the time of fertility had passed. Women were not to be confined to domesticity, but to participate in all aspects of society according to their abilities.

In the *Laws*, a dialogue written after Plato had tried without success to bring about his utopia, he reverts to a more complementary theory with separate education for men and women. What makes for order and purity in society is the feminine, and what leads to majesty and valor comes from the masculine. However, even in this second plan for society, Plato still wanted men and women both to learn gymnastics and horseback riding. Women were not to be treated like slaves. They were not to live softly and waste money, but instead to have reasonable order in their lives (Plato).

The first woman philosopher to write about the feminine, as far as we know, is Mary Wollstonecraft, an English woman of the eighteenth century. In *A Vindication of the Rights of Women*, Wollstonecraft tried to prove that what we have been calling negative feminine traits, far from being innate, are the result of the mores of society. Once these have been changed, the great positive virtues of women will emerge more and more clearly, as well as their equal claims to rationality, and hence to equal rights.

"It is time to separate unchangeable morals from local manners", Wollstonecraft thought, and to her morality meant living virtuously by Christian standards (Rossi 1973, 58). But to be ethical, a woman needed a different kind of education than the smattering that girls picked up in her day. She needed to understand principles, acquire rigor and discover causes rather than observe effects. Cool reason had to replace the reign of irrational romantic love.

Wollstonecraft believed that the kindly feminine traits

should come from true love, not submissive dependence. By means of a thorough intellectual and religious education, a woman would be as independent of spirit as a man, able to be a respected friend and confidant rather than a charming plaything. Such an upbringing would also make her a much better wife and mother.

John Stuart Mill also paved the way for English feminism. In his essay *On Liberty* (excerpted in Mahowald 1978), Mill claims that the real character of women is unknown since it has been so distorted by male philosophers with exploitative natures. It is to their advantage to teach women that they should live only for their husbands and children!

Although in Mill's time, women were treated like the body servants of despots, he looked forward to an age when marriage would be a union of equals. And, indeed, in his own marriage to an intellectual, equal rights were respected.

Although he thought most women would still want to be wives and mothers, even if this were not forced upon them by the customs of society, he thought it a loss to society if women were not able to exercise their other intellectual and creative faculties.

Mill agreed with his critics that women tended to be more intuitive than principled, but he taught that such imbalance was not innate but rather the result of an education deficient in analytic training. If there are few famous women in history, he noted, it is not due to lack of talent, but rather because women are bogged down with other duties.

Male supremacy has many disadvantages for society. Because of it, Mill argued, men grow to be arrogant and overbearing; the world loses the talents of women;

mothers, brought up themselves without a sufficient philosophical foundation, become poor educators of their own children; women keep men back from nonconformist activities for the reform of society, because they lack the breadth of vision to understand the needs of their times; social life becomes too dualistic, preventing the crossfertilization of ideas coming from both sexes.

At the end of the nineteenth century we find much agitation for women's rights. There is the Marxist viewpoint, stressing the way in which economic conditions lead to the exploitation of women. Engels wrote a long essay on the "Origin of the Family" (excerpted in Mahowald 1978), and Lenin's commentary was collected into a book entitled *The Emancipation of Women* (excerpted in Mahowald 1978). Engels thought that the women of the proletariat, even if they worked, were still domestic slaves and that the only way to bring about real equality was to abolish the family unit.

The women's suffrage movement became more militant in the early part of the twentieth century. In England such women as Emmeline Pankhurst chose to go to prison as a protest against the slowness of reform. Originally viewed as a proof of the silly naivete of women, this movement eventually proved the strength of its proponents.

The movement flourished also in the United States. Elizabeth Stanton and Lucretia Mott were already fighting for women's rights in 1848. Later, Susan B. Anthony became the leader. It is hard, in the 1980s, to believe that so many basic rights involving voting and property were denied solely on the basis of sex for so many centuries.

I mention these historical notes because some anti-feminists in our time act as if there never was any problem; they believe that feminism is only the ravings of crazed women of our era.

The most outstanding feminist voice of the twentieth century is the often quoted Simone de Beauvoir. Here is de Beauvoir's concise summary of her metaphysics as it relates to the plight of woman: Man transcends Life through existence, by this he creates values that deprive pure repetition of all value. In the animal the freedom and variety of male activities are vain because no project is involved. All is for the species. The human male remodels the face of the earth and shapes the future. The woman celebrates in festivals the victory of the males. Her misfortune is to have been biologically destined for the repetition of Life when even her own view of Life does not carry within itself its reason for being, reasons that are more important than the life itself (see de Beauvoir 1952, 59).

In other words, de Beauvoir thinks that having babies is merely a repetition, while men are able to do something new and original through their projects. Clearly, such a view differs tremendously from the presumably naive idea of many mothers: procreating a new human being is the greatest experience in life! Throughout *The Second Sex*, de Beauvoir contends that masculinity is the favored type, and femininity is secondary.

Women are afraid to risk establishing their own identity, and hence in their complicity with male dominance they develop the traits that work to the male's advantage. Men like to think women are happy in their stagnation. They delight in poetic images of the eternal feminine to conceal the monotony of maternity and domesticity.

Ethically, de Beauvoir rejects any condition that continues the limiting conditions of the past and present.

She links freedom with the search for change and identifies such liberty with the masculine personality. Women must be freed so that they can engage in projects of their own choice, without being subordinate to the men who surround them. The emancipated woman wants to be a taker and a doer, not a passive object of male needs.

Yet, de Beauvoir says, the contemporary woman finds herself in an ambiguous position. On the one hand, she wants to hold on to her feminine ways of manipulating men, and on the other hand she wants to assert her equal transcendence. ·

It would seem that de Beauvoir's solution to the tension between femininity and freedom is to opt for freedom and get rid of the feminine. However, a close reading of *The Second Sex* shows that it is primarily the negative feminine which she rejects. She will endorse the positive feminine, provided it is not viewed as innate but as a choice. This metaphysics rejects the concept of creation as a gift.

De Beauvoir's ideal is comradeship between men and women. This can be brought about, not merely by economic changes, but by embodying new values in cultural forms such as family and education. This will eliminate feminine dependence and inferiority, but need not banish "love, happiness, poetry, dream".

In spite of egalitarian statements made in the past, today's feminists can point to the long tradition in Western philosophy and culture that expressed negativity toward women.

Although some of the most frequently quoted excerpts that demonstrate this bias are taken out of context and can be nuanced by other quotations, it is important to refer to a few, just to see how they cause feminist ire.

Aristotle, a disciple of Plato, was convinced that women were inferior to men. In *Generation of Animals*, he wrote: "A female is a defective male." In *Poetics* he wrote that it was unseemly to portray a woman as manly or clever. (Both are excerpted in Mahowald 1978.)

Rousseau explains in *Emile* that men should be active and strong; women passive, weak and pleasing to men.

In "On Women" from *Studies in Pessimism* (excerpted in Mahowald 1978), Schopenhauer describes men as objective and strong, but women as unable to perform anything requiring great labor. She pays her debt to life by suffering, sacrifice and submission. Men are capable of keen joys and sorrows, women of more trivial things. Men are adult, women are big children. Men are able to consider the past and future and hence develop the virtue of prudence and justice. Men are in every respect superior to women. Men, their reason clouded by sexual desire, foolishly think of women as the fairer sex, whereas in actuality women are "undersized, narrow-shouldered, broad-hipped, and short-legged". According to Schopenhauer, women are rightly called the second sex, "inferior in every respect to the first". They should be denied legal rights.

Nietzsche composed such aphorisms as, "Thou goest to a woman? Remember thy whip!" And, "When a woman has scholarly inclinations there is generally something wrong with her sexual nature."

The philosophy of Jean-Paul Sartre, the famous existentialist of our century, presents us with quite a different, though equally repulsive, manner of describing feminine traits. In Sartre's metaphysics nature is seen as absurd, as nauseating. Without God, there is no meaning to existence. God's creation appears to Sartre only as a sort of slime. Love is viewed as a process of destructive appropriation of the freedom of another, and sex is seen as nothing but the emission of slimy substances for the relief of physical pressure.

Here is a vivid description of slime as characteristic of all nature, and peculiarly of feminine nature:

> I open my hands, I want to let go of the slimy and it sticks to me, it drowns me, it sucks at me. . . . It is a soft, yielding action, a moist and feminine sucking, it lives obscurely under my finger, and I sense it like a dizziness; it draws me to it as the bottom of a precipice might draw me. . . . Slime is the revenge of the In-itself [unconscious being], a sickly sweet feminine revenge which will be symbolized on another level by the quality of "sugary" . . . a sugary sliminess is the ideal of the slimy; it symbolizes the sugary death of the For-itself [conscious being] like that of the wasp which sinks into the jam and drowns in it (Sartre 1957, 609).

And further on in the same section of his existential metaphysical tome, *Being and Nothingness*, Sartre again describes the feminine:

> Here at its origin we grasp one of the most fundamental tendencies of human reality—the tendency to fill. . . . A good part of our life is passed in plugging up holes, in filling empty places, in realizing and symbolically establishing a plenitude. . . . It is only from this standpoint that we can pass on to sexuality. The obscenity of the feminine sex is that of everything which "gapes open". It is an appeal to being, as all holes are. In herself woman appeals to a strange flesh which is to transform her into a fullness of being by penetration and dissolution. Conversely woman senses her condition as an appeal precisely because she is "in the form of a hole". . . .

Beyond any doubt her sex is a mouth and a voracious mouth which devours the penis—a fact which can easily lead to the idea of castration. The amorous act is the castration of the man; but this is above all because sex is a hole. We have to do here with a presexual contribution which will become one of the components of sexuality as an empirical, complex, human attitude but which far from deriving its origin from the sexed being has nothing in common with basic sexuality. . . . Nevertheless the experience with the hole . . . includes the ontological presentiment of sexual experience in general. . . . The hole, before all sexual specification, is an obscene expectation, an appeal to the flesh (Sartre 1957, 613–614).

I include this horrifying description of the feminine by Sartre in order to show how far the rejection of God and nature in general can lead to rejection of the feminine nature.

Our discussion of feminism proceeds with a brief survey of comments from contemporary writers.

The book that triggered the women's liberation movement in the United States was *The Feminine Mystique*, written in 1963 by Betty Friedan. This best-selling paperback described the frustrations of middle-class suburban housewives. The anger it created in women who were jerked out of their passivity by Friedan's depiction of their plight helped to swell the numbers who would eventually support the more militant aims of such women's liberation organizations as NOW.

Let's consider some of the ideas Friedan wrote in "Our Revolution is Unique" (excerpted in Mahowald 1978), after her own movement had split—the more radical members claimed that Friedan was too moderate.

"Man is not the enemy, but the fellow victim of the

present half-equality." His residual negativity deprives him of the sensitivity and tenderness he, himself, longs to express.

On the subject of sex and related issues, Friedan claims that women will only cease to be sex objects "when they are liberated to a creativity beyond motherhood, to a full human creativity". Motherhood is good, but only when chosen freely. According to Friedan, the right to contraceptives and abortion is crucial for the liberation of women.

However, Friedan's controversial and, to me, horrifying, acceptance of contraception and abortion as essential elements in a feminist program seems like a mild voice in comparison to her radical sisters from whose writings we will now give samples.

Some writers think that the institution of marriage "protects" women in the same way that the institution of slavery was said to "protect" blacks—that is, the word "protection" in this case is simply a euphemism for oppression. Freedom for women cannot be won without abolition of marriage (Koedt and Firestone 1971).

The articles in the Second Year's annual of the same series develop this theme: it is necessary to destroy love, for love prevents the full development of a woman's human potential by directing all her energies outward in the interest of others.

As we proceed to more and more extreme variations on the theme of radical change, you will note the vehemence of tone, culminating in manifestos where the proliferation of four-letter words (negative masculine?) seemed to me to require some censorship in the form of omissions to avoid offense.

Along these lines let me begin with quotations from

the writing of Ti-Grace Atkinson from *Amazon Odyssey* (excerpted in Mahowald 1978).

Traditional feminism failed, Atkinson theorizes, because it didn't get to the root of the problem—the tendency of women to define themselves in terms of masculine society. What is needed is for women to "eradicate their own definition. Women must, in a sense, commit suicide. . . . As women begin massing together, they take the first step from *being* massacred to *engaging in* battle (resistance). Hopefully this will eventually lead to negotiations—in the very far future—and peace."

This was written in the 60s. When she resigned from NOW Atkinson thought that women must reject marriage and love and sex as well. In this way women can begin to define themselves without reference to being the "wife-man of a husband or the suckler [female] of a baby".

It is not men that must be destroyed but rather their learned roles—oppressive roles which she described as "metaphysical cannibalism", i.e., appropriating women into a slave position. Why do men try to cannibalize women? All people—men and women—feel frustrated by their own lack of complete power and so they seek to gain some degree of control through enslaving others. In the case of men, the exploitation is direct, for a man can literally enter a woman and occupy her body. This is a form of rape, according to Ti-Grace Atkinson.

How can a woman escape such tyranny? Does she even wish to? Atkinson describes woman's traditional way of avoiding confrontation with her weak passivity as "the psychopathological condition of love".

It is a euphoric state of fantasy in which the victim transforms her oppressor into her redeemer. She turns her natural hostility toward the aggressor against the remnants of herself—her Consciousness—and sees her

counterpart in contrast to herself as all-powerful [as he
is by now at her expense]. . . . What is . . . necessary is
for the Oppressed to cure themselves [destroy the female
role], to throw off the Oppressor, and to help the
Oppressor to cure himself [to destroy the male role].

Selections from a chapter in the anthology *Masculine/
Feminine*, edited by Betty and Theodore Roszak (1969),
give expression to a feminism increasingly dominated by
negative masculine rhetoric and suggesting that the only
way to overcome weakness and to be free is to become
brutal.

The WITCH *Manifesto*

On Halloween 1963 women guerrillas dressed as witches
and descended on the New York Stock Exchange heaping
curses and spells upon high finance and singing a song
especially written for the occasion, "Up Against the
Wall Street". "The WITCH Manifesto" is another expression of this vociferous and theatrical group—or should
we say coven?

WITCH is in all women, everything.
It's theatre, revolution,
Magic, terror and joy.
It's an awareness that witches and gypsies
Were the first guerrillas and resistance fighters
Against oppression—the oppression of women,
Down through the ages.
Witches have always been women who dared
To be groovy, courageous, aggressive,
Intelligent, non-conformist, explorative,
Independent, sexually liberated, and revolutionary.
(This may explain why nine million women

Have been burned as witches.)
Witches were the first friendly heads
   and dealers,
The first birth-control practitioners,
   and abortionists,
The first alchemists.
They bowed to no man,
Being the last living remnants
Of the oldest culture of all—
One in which men and women are equal
sharers in a truly cooperative society,
Before the death-dealing sexual,
Economic, and spiritual repression
Of the "Imperialist Phallic Society"
Took over and began to s—— all over nature,
And human life.

A witch lives and laughs in every woman.
She is the free part of each of us,
Beneath the shy smiles,
The acquiescence to absurd male domination,
The make-up of flesh-suffocating clothing
Our sick society demands.
There is no joining WITCH.
If you are a woman, and dare to look within yourself,
You are a witch.
You make your own rules.
You are free and beautiful.
You can be invisible or evident,
In how you choose to make your witch self known.
You can form your own Coven of sister witches.
Do your own actions.
Whatever is repressive,
Solely male-oriented,
Greedy, puritanical, authoritarian,
Those are your targets,

Your weapons are theatre,
Magic, satire, explosions, herbs,
Music, costumes, masks, stickers,
Paint, brooms, voodoo dolls,
Cats, candles, bells,
Your boundless beautiful imagination.
Your power comes from your own self,
As a woman.
From sharing, rapping, and acting
In concert with your sisters.
You are pledged to free our brothers
From oppression and stereotyped sexual roles,
as well as ourselves.
You are a witch by being female,
Untamed, angry, joyous and immortal.
You are a witch by saying aloud
"I am a witch"
And thinking about that.

If this manifesto seems so utterly wild to you that you would never expect to meet anyone with such views, consider that *some*, though certainly *not* all, Christian feminists wish to introduce pagan symbols into the Mass. A conference calling itself "Christian feminist" ended with a liberating dance by all those present who exulted in their lesbianism.

One last "gem" comes from "The Bitch Manifesto" (anonymous 1969 [unpublished]), and it is included to indicate an extreme of how feminist assertiveness might manifest itself as an antidote to passivity:

Bitches are aggressive, assertive, domineering, over-bearing, strong-minded, spiteful, hostile, direct, blunt, candid, obnoxious, thick-skinned, hard-headed, vicious, dogmatic, competent, competitive, pushy, independent, stubborn, demanding, manipulative, egoistic, driven, achieving, overwhelming, threatening, scary, ambitious, tough, brassy, masculine, boisterous, and turbulent. Among other things, a Bitch occupies a lot of psychological space. You always know when she is around. . . . You may not like her, but you cannot ignore her.

The Truths of Feminism

For some readers, no doubt, the final excerpts of the preceding section would considerably diminish any interest in hearing about the truths of feminism. Others have found even radical feminism peculiarly stimulating, hiding truth even in the midst of exaggeration or false ethical principles.

What then do I believe to be the truths of feminism? They can be divided into four basic aspects: the rejection of the negative masculine exploitation of women because of the equal dignity of persons; the rejection of the negative feminine with all its degrading compromises; the rejection of stereotyping in favor of individual freedom; and the development of programs for social change.

A report of the World Synod of Catholic Bishops of 1980 (*Origins*, Oct. 23, 1980) includes the following points:

> In point of fact, there is no reputable theologian today who would deny that the equality of man and woman is constituted by God and confirmed by Christian teaching. . . . In many cultures women are discriminated against in one way or another and left in a subservient, dominant and competitive role. . . . At the same time,

under the influence of the Holy Spirit, people around the world are becoming more and more sensitive to the dignity of each person, regardless of sex, creed and race, recognizing the person's innate right to respect and freedom from unjust oppression. . . . The state of submission and oppression which women are subjected to in the world is a sinful situation, the result of original sin . . . therefore, something to correct.

Both the feminist movement and the hippie movement of the 60s and 70s exposed the evils of negative masculine traits such as domineering, smug and patronizing attitudes. Men eager to show their rejection of the negative masculine are quick to volunteer to pour coffee at a meeting, to plan the menu and to cook. Fewer now refer to middle-aged women as girls. Many more men share family duties with their working wives. Men are learning the value of showing emotion and vulnerability.

I also applaud feminism's rejection of certain aspects of the negative feminine such as overdependence, silliness, coyness, naiveté, manipulativeness, random seductiveness and compulsive chatter.

There is a great need for strong women. Weak feminine types may be charming in certain respects, but not in an embattled time of conflict.

In her work on woman's education, the Catholic philosopher Edith Stein wrote:

By nature, women have the gifts to pursue non-domestic tasks. It is only reasonable and in accordance with nature to transcend the circle of domestic duties where this is too narrow to allow of a full development of one's gifts. The limit beyond which we may not go, however, seems to me to be reached if the professional activities endanger the domestic life, that is the educational community of parents and children (Stein 1956, 121).

I particularly appreciate this emphasis on the individual and her special talents which is developing as a result of feminist pressure. I personally have no great interest in traditionally masculine sports, but why not delight when other women enjoy them and can successfully compete. As Simone de Beauvoir correctly perceived, girls do not climb trees to be equal to boys, they do so because it's fun! Why shouldn't women logicians, engineers or doctors follow their natural bents? In the past, women with temperaments less suited to the duties of life in the home were often reduced to seething resentment, as they felt forced to fulfill hated tasks day after day.

Without agreeing with some feminists who think of full-time day care as the career mom's final solution, I do believe that feminist social programs can benefit a woman who wants to combine motherhood with other activities on a part-time basis.

In my classes in philosophy of women I find that the issue of motherhood versus career is the greatest cause of stress for my women students. Many think that there is no way to combine both a career and motherhood; they fantasize that they can achieve some kind of perfection only if they pursue one or the other without distraction. Hence they face these frightening alternatives: either to pursue a career and use contraceptives or abortion, experiencing uncreative sexual happiness along the way or to choose the mother role and squelch their desire for other forms of self-expression.

A career-mother myself, I am anxious to present to

such students a variety of other approaches to their dilemma. Here is the information I give to them:

Some alternatives for working or nonworking mothers

The role of full-time homemaker may be crucial only up to the year that the children are all in school. Then the mother can combine her homemaker role with part-time or full-time work elsewhere.

Some of the duties traditionally performed by the mother can be performed by the husband, children or outside helpers, freeing her for other roles.

The roles of homemaking can be considered so crucial and all encompassing that they ought to be shared by male and female, as a half-time job for each.

The role of homemaking is crucial but can be held as a full-time job by another person in the home, for example a live-in nanny or a relative.

The role of homemaker can be reduced. Parents and children can spend the least possible time on chores, live simply, eat out as much as possible, thereby enabling both parents to work outside at their chosen jobs.

There need be no set plan for all families. There can be different phases such as the following:

Phase one: Wife works and husband gets a degree; husband takes care of children.

Phase two: Husband works, wife finishes her degree and takes care of the children with help of part-time nursery.

Phase three: Both work part-time and spend a lot of time with family or both work full-time and hire a live-in nanny.

Alternative:

Phase one: Both work.

Phase two: One or other stops working to raise children until all are in school, could be combined with part-time work or part-time development of creative talents, community and parish work, further schooling, etc.

Phase three: The parent who stayed home works full-time and other parent retires early to pursue part-time work or other interests.

Other Alternatives:

Some possible principles for choices for both men and women:

1. Do what is most fulfilling for oneself, yet moral and legal, and hope that this will eventually work out best for all. Then avoid "buying into guilt trips laid on you by others".

2. Do what you think is best for all of the family and pursue individual goals on a long-term basis as you can.

3. Consult with a counsellor or wise friend to guard oneself against possible rationalizations.

4. Determine the long-term life goals and a philosophy of the meaning of life for both husband and wife. Make other decisions in line with this philosophy even if these decisions are psychologically or financially difficult at the time. Get as much support as possible from people who believe in the same life goals.

5. Experiment!

Let us return to the truths of feminism. The delightful and poignant essay *A Room of One's Own*, by Virginia

Woolf describes how much the creative woman has been hampered in the past by her living arrangements. While middle-class men usually worked in their own study, women writers and artists would pull their equipment out of a closet and work amidst the joyful or painful screaming of their children.

I dream of a time when, with the help of my feminist sisters, every living and working area will include a well-staffed child-care center with access to a communal cafeteria. I would love to see our society support stipends for mothers, which were recommended by Pope John Paul II, so that no woman would ever decide against having children for economic reasons. I dream of maternity and paternity leave. I dream of an abundance of grants for married women to support part-time study for degrees.

Lastly, I have found it tremendously helpful to communicate with other women about their problems and their successes, both in the home and at work, in the forms that have come out of the feminist movement. More and more we are reading fiction and nonfiction written by women and depicting the lives of women.

Falsehoods and False Values of Feminism

My critique of feminism will include the following main points: most feminism uses the masculine as a model, thereby underrating the positive feminine; while early feminists considered abortion a result of the negative masculine irresponsibility of the male, most contemporary feminists endorse this act, which is the most rampant abuse of the innocent in our society today; lastly, I will try to show that most feminism lacks a philosophy of the person from which to ground the positive feminine.

In my comments on the ideas of radical feminists, I have already begun to indicate the distressing manner in which women, originally protesting negative masculine traits in men, now slide into recommending them for women.

Christine Garside Allen, in an unpublished article "True Sex-Polarity", mentions that in all revolutions there can be distortions, especially when the newly freed group takes on the characteristics of the oppressor. In this case, the revolution commits suicide.

We are all familiar with the increasing number of aggressive, shrewd, cold and domineering women to be found in our society since the promotion of militant feminism.

Contemporary norms in the education and acculturation of women can also present the problem of the disparagement of the positive feminine in terms of the development of positive and negative masculine qualities.

Many times the legitimate seeking of equality leads to a sameness of education often, though by no means always, along masculine lines. More women are being steered into fields previously dominated by men, than men are being encouraged to study homemaking skills. To trace this idea back to its foundation in feminism, consider this: Why does de Beauvoir see interior decorating as drudgery yet building a community fountain, say, as exhilarating? Psychologist Judith Bardwick (1979) writes that all too often women internalize male roles and also their criteria for success and achievement such as competence, risk taking and competitiveness. Instead, we might be judging ourselves on how cooperative we were, how willing to affirm others in a work situation, as some feminists do recommend.

Ethical issues related to feminism are significantly related to the depreciation of the positive feminine coming out of the women's liberation movement. 1973 saw the lowest birthrate and the highest divorce rate in the history of America according to Samuel Blumenfeld in his book *The Retreat from Motherhood* (1975). Women are losing the sense of the privilege of motherhood. He suggests also that men often support women's liberation because it allows them to be more irresponsible. Women, persuaded that marriage and family life are imprisoning, will not wait for marriage for their sexual fulfillment.

Browsing through a stationery store one day, I was interested in the amount of space, almost half, devoted to the sale of stuffed animals of an astounding variety. I noticed that girls and women, after purchasing these cute toys, would hug the animal to their breasts. Some women I know have whole beds full of individually named stuffed animals on which they lavish the affection they might be extending to the live babies they have rejected by contraception and abortion.

In a kind of manifesto I once wrote: I long for the day when feminists will realize that equal rights for women need not be accompanied by negation of the distinctly feminine.

What kind of freedom is it that insists on using contraceptive devices harmful to women's bodies and often also abortifacient?

Doesn't it show more self-love and strength to demand that men respect the special fertile time when we are potential mothers?

I would like to see the day when knowledge of our

own natural cycles will enable us to proclaim with pride, "This week I am a potential miracle worker. Come to me with your seed only if you want to be part of this wonder by becoming a father!"

I would like to see the day when no woman would punish herself, her man or her baby by abortion, but would instead cherish her own womb and its fruit. For isn't abortion a form of stereotyping when it speaks of unwanted babies instead of affirming the uniqueness of each baby? And is it not an extreme form of negative masculine control to pass a death sentence on a helpless infant because he or she will not be an asset at this time? I would like to see the day when all women would avail themselves of the help offered by the prolife community to overcome any financial, psychological or other difficulties that stand in the way of completing their motherhood.

I would like to see "sisterhood become powerful": women who could not raise their children would bear them courageously to give to their nonfertile sisters in adoption. I would like to see women working together for maternity and paternity leave, better day care and for creative ways to combine motherhood and careers.

Is true feminism antilife? No. Can a feminist support the Human Life Amendment? Yes. As a wife, mother and professional woman I look forward to the day when all women will see that affirming their own lives means affirming the lives of all, no matter how small!

Are the defects of feminism correctable? That is a most controversial question. I do believe that there can be a philosophy of woman that includes feminism's valid insights about freedom. But such a viewpoint would have to include a metaphysical foundation in which to ground the positive feminine.

Let me try to explain what I mean in simple terms. All values find their home in the nature of reality. Freedom depends on objectivity. Our theoretical notion of what is the most basic meaning of life enables us to sort out various values and determine priorities.

If, for example, the meaning of life is self-fulfillment through the development of one's physical, intellectual and artistic abilities—exclusively—then the development of positive feminine values is but a possibility; such values will be considered good if they foster individuality, bad if they impede it.

But suppose, instead, that the meaning of life is growth in love. Then the experiences of the heart in most intimate relationships will be of equal if not superior value to cultivation of other gifts; and, for a woman, the use of her special forms of relating will be cherished as prime. She will want not only freedom to choose, but liberty to have strength to sustain womanly roles. And her loving-ness will also free the male sex to be responsible and fathering instead of cold and uncaring.

In other words, to be truly free as a woman one must also be feminine and faithful.

WHOLENESS

Another theory about how to liberate women to greater strength is called wholeness. This philosophy is hard to define and survey because it is both relatively new and also so fertile with new insights and combinations that its parameters are quite difficult to discover. Let me begin then by simply defining wholeness theory as it will be used in this chapter. *Wholeness* is a goal of personality growth by which the feminine and masculine components are integrated in both women and men.

Wholeness springs from the perception, developed primarily in Jungian psychology, that many people are one-sided in some respects, including the masculine or feminine. A man might have too much masculine and too little feminine. A woman might have too much feminine and too little masculine. But also a man might have too much feminine or a woman too much masculine. Psychic wholeness comes when such imbalances begin to be rectified by "coming into touch with" the deeply hidden and undeveloped parts of the self.

The discussion of feminine and masculine in Jungian psychology includes two terms, which are still quite vague and confusing to the uninitiated, the *anima* and the *animus*. These words are not, as some imagine, simply synonyms for feminine and masculine. No. They are more subtle. They are archetypes: inherited modes of psychic functioning that parallel certain instincts in animals.

As defined by the Jungian analyst Esther Harding (1971), *anima* is the feminine part of a man's nature, unconscious to him, and usually projected; *animus* is the masculine part of a woman's nature.

In other words, every man has an archetypal image of the feminine, a highly emotionally charged fantasy symbol. This "feminine principle" is really inside him, but he projects it onto real women, as he tries to find the ideal in the real. In the same way, every woman has an

archetypal image of the masculine. This masculine principle is within her, but is projected onto the men she
meets, as she seeks the ideal in the real.

Here is the way Jung (1875–1961) expressed it in his
own fascinating if less clear manner of writing:

> Every man carries within him the eternal image of woman,
> not the image of this or that particular woman, but a
> definite feminine image. This image is fundamentally
> unconscious, a hereditary factor of primordial origin
> engraved in the living organic system of the man, an
> imprint or archetype of all the ancestral experiences of the
> female, a deposit, as it were, of all the impressions ever
> made by woman—in short an inherited system of psychic
> adaptation. . . . The same is true of woman: she, too, has
> her inborn image of man. . . . Since this image is uncon-
> scious, it is always unconsciously projected upon the
> person of the beloved, and is one of the chief reasons for
> passionate attraction or aversion.

Projection ultimately fails, for real men and women
cannot satisfy our desire for the perfection of the ideal.
However, all is not lost. When, in the course of therapy,
or self-analysis, a man or woman realizes the extent of
his or her yearning for the feminine or masculine, he or
she may begin to search for it within the *self*.

So, for example, if I find myself passionately in love
with a man because of his obvious strength, and then
become disillusioned when I discover his clay feet, instead of turning against the man in bitterness because he
failed to be an adequate leaning post, I can seek the
masculine strength I need within my own self.

Or, if I am a man who is enchanted and fixated on a
delicate, tender woman and then feel cheated to discover
that she is not a flower but a live human being, capable

even of perspiration, instead of punishing her for failing to live up to my image, I can seek the delicate tender emotions buried within my own psyche, for example, by writing poetry or tending a garden.

How do these ideas about projection of the masculine and feminine relate to wholeness theory? Becoming aware that there are hidden masculine and feminine parts of myself, I can try to become whole, or integrated, by getting in touch with these parts. The whole man will then *live out* his masculine and feminine traits. The whole woman will be comfortable with *living out* her feminine and masculine traits.

To make this idea more vivid, think of women and men you admire. Do not most of them have this kind of wholeness? Christian Jungians advise us to meditate on the way that Jesus manifested all the masculine and feminine traits. Was Joan of Arc not passionately responsive and yet also courageous to the death?

In relation to our discussion of weak women seeking the roots of freedom through greater strength, let's see what a Jungian wholeness analyst might think about this process. M. Esther Harding writes:

> Western civilization lays a special emphasis on the value of the outer, and this fits in more nearly with man's nature than with woman's. The feminine spirit is more subjective, more concerned with feelings and relationships than with the laws and principles of the outer world. And so it happens that the conflict between outer and inner is usually more devastating for women than for men (Harding 1971, 10).

According to Harding, there is a great conflict in women between the masculine side they must develop in order to work in the world, and their "more ancient feminine nature". For women of our times "a one-sided life is not sufficient; the conflict between the opposing tendencies of masculine and feminine within them must be faced. They cannot resume the feminine values in the old instinctive and unconscious way."

Harding thinks that modern women are more schooled in the masculine than the feminine and that they will be stronger by relating to their feminine side!

In an interesting chapter in *Woman's Mysteries*, Harding develops the concept of "The Virgin Goddess" as a symbol of a feminine way of being liberated. The virgin goddesses in various religions are not dependent on a human male, but achieve fulfillment by being ravished by their god. Meditation on virgin goddesses can lead women to understand the way in which sacrifices of the ego's desires can be freeing and renewing when our passions are given back to the God to whom we belong. Through the transformation of passion in response to the divine, women can gain sexual control without the unsatisfactory effects of repression. Out of such unconventional sublimation of sexual drives comes the maternal feeling women desire so keenly to experience with a universal scope. In other words, we cannot just repress the negative feminine, for then it will always come back in haunting fantasies and destructive outbreaks. Instead, we must relate to the divine in complete passion and let the divine fertilize us, bringing forth positive feminine traits.

In relation to the problem of possessiveness, Harding points to the archetype of the goddesses who have to sacrifice their sons. Today women who ponder such symbols will come to understand the primordial meaning of the necessary process of letting go.

A woman healed and integrated through the divine can inspire men without trying to conquer them. If she is married, her *inner* virginity will express itself in her independence of convention and ratification by others. She will be a free spirit or, in Jung's terms, an *individual* who is at home in herself.

Receiving Woman, a book by Ann Belford Ulanov (1981), another Jungian therapist and Professor of Psychiatry and Religion at Union Theological Seminary, can aid our further understanding of the ideal of wholeness and feminine strength.

Reacting against the stereotyping of the past and also of present-day movements, Ulanov tries to help each woman see herself as an individual with a wide range of possibilities as she combines the masculine and feminine parts of herself.

> Many women are beginning to understand that they can no more be determined in their inmost selves by the old benevolent patriarchy than by the new malevolent sexism. New stereotypes are no less coercive than old ones. No great distance exists between "All real women marry and bear children" and "All real women know that men are sexists and rapists at heart." In both, woman is a passive victim determined by forces outside herself that she may resist, but is all but helpless to change (Ulanov 1981, 17).

Unlike Jung, Ulanov objects to the idea that woman experiences her unconscious as masculine in the obverse of the way man finds his unconscious to be feminine. Instead she feels that our concept of the feminine has to expand to include all of what women really are, including intellect, drive and power.

The idea that women become strong, not by trying to be more masculine, but by allowing their own individual freedom and courage to come forth, is becoming more prevalent among psychologists. After all, gentleness is different in a man than in a woman precisely because it is a powerful man who is being gentle. In the same way, strength in a woman is different precisely because it may overcome passivity.

In *The Woman in the Tower* by Betsy Caprio (1983), a spiritual director and parish minister, women are taught to experiment with possibilities of greater wholeness by getting in touch with the four elements, symbols of Jungian personality types.

> Air = thinking
> Earth = sensory
> Fire = intuition
> Water = feeling

With regard to the feminine and masculine, Caprio resolves a problem I have often puzzled over in my study of wholeness theory. If women develop the masculine and men the feminine, why wouldn't their personalities end up being alike? Then it would make no difference whether one was with a woman or a man except biologically! Betsy Caprio theorizes, on the contrary, that for a woman to be whole she must develop her feminine side *first*. The masculine in her must take the form of *inner* strength and not become an aggressive thrust in the world. Likewise, for men, the masculine must be developed first, with the feminine flourishing within, rather than in an outward form of exaggerated feminine traits.

In terms of the categories developed in this book, one could say that in Caprio's image the woman would have a strong positive feminine bolstered by an inner positive masculine, and the man would have a strong positive masculine with a beautiful inner positive feminine. If the woman tries to develop the masculine first, she is all too likely to fall into the negative masculine. If the man tries to develop the feminine first, he may slip into the negative feminine.

Jungians also speak of women having different personality types, each with its own strengths. The girlish woman is spontaneous and charming; the interior woman has the strength of wisdom. The motherly woman is enduring; the amazon can carry out projects in the world at large. One can gain in wholeness by developing areas of the feminine previously neglected.

Strengths of Wholeness Theory

I become most aware of the truths of wholeness theory when I meet an individual who demonstrates a remarkable lack of wholeness: for instance an extremely negative masculine man who is cold, domineering and overly critical; or an extraordinarily negative feminine woman who is weak, passive and silly. And so, I consider one of the main strengths of the concept of wholeness to be the attempt to liberate people from such crippling one-sidedness.

Another benefit of wholeness theory is the reverence its proponents exhibit for the processes going on in the deeper part of others as well as oneself.

Most women can truly be one-sidedly feminine at times and this can severely limit their freedom to bring about the good. There are circumstances in which feminine warmth, charm and intuition need the balance of a daring attitude, leadership and objectivity that comes from analysis.

The word "process" has become something of a cliche in popular psychology, along with its correlative "growth". Yet we owe a great deal to the thinkers who have developed such concepts. A Christian button worn in the 70s read "Please don't judge me; God hasn't finished working on me yet."

The belief that others and oneself are not fixed in unsatisfactory patterns, but instead might be in a state of hibernation pending a new spring, helps bring forth new energies. In a novel Charles Williams once had a sage advise his neophyte that it was a sin to give up on another person, to make a picture of him at his worst moment and then believe that to be the final portrait. Juli Loesch, columnist for the *National Catholic Register*, often warns against "hard-boiling" people in their sins.

Sister Mary Neill, a Dominican theologian who is well versed in wholeness theory, gives many self-exploration workshops. She uses common images to jostle the psyche out of its rut-like resignation to stagnant patterns. Questions such as, "When have you most needed a refuge?" and "When have you been a refuge for others?" gently lead the participant into openness to positive feminine and masculine traits. Sister Neill sometimes speaks of those whose personalities seem consolidated around negative characteristics as "not having done their emotional homework".

In other words, we should not think we can become Amazons just by an exercise of will power, but neither should we sink into passivity about our shortcomings.

Reverence for our struggles to achieve wholeness leads us to appreciate the individual instead of insisting on conformity. Proposals for flexible options in society can be offered in a warm concerned way, rather than in the strident, protesting spirit sometimes displayed by feminists who push the same programs.

Weaknesses of Wholeness Theory

The weaknesses of wholeness theory become apparent when wholeness is considered the sole goal of life. When its insights are instead part of a wider philosophy, especially a Christian perspective, the defects of this psychological school can be overcome, for the most part.

The problems I see in wholeness theory include these: insufficient distinction between positive and negative traits, idolization of process and of the individual, vagueness about critical ethical norms.

Some proponents of wholeness theory will refer to certain traits as demonic, but very often the interest in overcoming repression takes the form of a fascination with the feminine and masculine without distinguishing between the positive and negative traits of each.

A therapeutic perspective can influence an individual's philosophy in a way that may confuse rather than clarify the issues. Since the unexpressed parts of the personality can explode destructively, therapists may advise clients to experiment with their hidden masculine or feminine. The result can be worse than the original less dynamic, but less harmful, state of being. For example, a masculinized woman may start manifesting her negative feminine by seducing happily married men. A quiet, passive man may become viciously violent as he explores his repressed masculine.

M. Esther Harding reveals something of this problem. On the one hand, she seems to praise the irrational, and on the other, she warns against it.

Mystical symbols of the feminine and masculine speak to us with enormous power: "Their strange nonrational logic will carry its own conviction and no rational proof of their truth will be necessary" (Harding 1971, 38; *see also* 81–82). Yet, in Harding's chapter on the virgin goddess, she warns against displacing conventionality with egocentricity when letting loose in the sensual realm. Genuine love most be safeguarded as a prime value.

It is easy to see how the lack of a clear distinction between negative and positive traits can lead to vagueness about ethical norms and the commitments involved. It is not uncommon to hear women involved in the imagery of wholeness justify experimental sexual activity, contraception, abortion, divorce or leaving their children by saying that they are just not "ready" for the full commitment required to be a wife or a mother. But such decisions deeply wound the feminine.

Homosexuality, as a lifestyle as well as an orientation, is sometimes also justified as an opportunity to explore the feminine or masculine side of a personality.

Such ambiguity or deviance from Christian moral norms, even among religious people immersed in wholeness theory, reflects the tendency to make the individual and his processes into a sort of absolute, or idol, to which others may have to be sacrificed.

For instance, Jungian analyst Ann Ulanov, in *Receiving Woman*, describes new ways that women are seeking themselves. She writes:

A woman in her fifties leaves her marriage of many years because she knows it to have been a pretense that damaged both parties and their children. She is not at all certain who she is or where she belongs. By seizing the outer truth she hopes to find her way to the inner one. Though criticized by her ex-husband as selfish in her action of divorce, she believes she gives a gift to him and to their children: an example, even if confused and groping, of trying to live out who one truly is. She finds this less painful and more live-giving than persisting in a false identity (Ulanov 1981, 28).

A more drastic example is given in Doris Lessing's *Children of Violence* (1970). A girl brought up in a puritanical household becomes wild in her teens. Then she seeks security in a conventional marriage. But she finds being a mother to be stifling, in spite of the ample help of servants and other luxuries of her middle-class South African life. While her daughter is still a young child, she abruptly abandons her home to seek fulfillment through immersion in Communist activities.

Returning to Ann Ulanov's example, she does not claim that divorce is good in itself. This would not be the way a wholeness theorist would express herself. Instead, she leaves out the moral question entirely, and makes the individual's exploration of the destiny of self more important.

Giving such absolute value to the individual often accompanies a tendency to view the divine, not as a Trinity of really existing Persons, but rather as images that symbolize the nameless transcendent. Harding writes of the virginity of Mary as one of a number of instances of virgin goddess symbols. The factual validity of this doctrine is not proposed but rather is left vague.

Yet I maintain that such a lack of clarity about the objectivity of Divine Persons actually militates against the complete feminine experience that Jungians are so eager to foster. Trustful, peaceful surrender to the Divine Persons depends upon faith. Otherwise a certain non-directional inwardness in prayer and meditation contributes to negative feminine self-absorption.

A similar problem can arise in close relationships between women and men because of the idolization of the process. In a very subtle manner people can view members of the opposite sex, not as unique lovable personalities in themselves, but instead as stepping stones, as the means to fostering an individual's psychological processes. "He brings out the feminine in me; that's why I love him." "She brings out the masculine in me; that's why I love her." The language of projection can make it appear that the beloved has no independent qualities whatsoever, as in such expressions as, "You are projecting your inner masculine on that man." Is he just a blank slate ready to be projected on? Of course not, but the lack of a full metaphysics of the precious goodness of the person can impede the woman's grateful response to the real qualities of the other, depriving her of one part of the positive feminine experience of affirmation.

Others question whether targeting feminine or masculine qualities, such as nurturing or freedom, is the way to reach them. Participating in many different kinds of human potential workshops can create the illusion that one can arrive at wholeness through persistent experimentation and introspection. But often such desired traits arise more naturally through responding to the challenges of life. For example, a woman who has never heard of methods for bringing out her femininity may realize it simply by carrying a baby to term. Her tender, empathetic characteristics will emerge in response to the baby rather than as a result of artificial methods. Similarly, a man or woman may develop leadership traits by accepting new responsibilities rather than by joining consciousness raising groups.

In general, the wholeness model fosters a somewhat misleading image of the strong woman who seeks her own salvation by means of a series of courageous interior adventures. This risk taking sounds wonderful, particularly in contrast to the mindless way many of us are formed by a value-anemic culture. What is left out, however, is our ultimate vulnerable dependency on God and other loving persons for the discovery of the deepest meaning of our lives. How such faith in God will fulfill the dream of feminine and free will be the subject of the final section.

FREEDOM TRANSFIGURED IN FAITH

Faith in a God of love who sacrificed himself for us to open the doors of heaven naturally leads to greater freedom. "The truth shall set you free."

Spontaneity and daring are impeded by fear, but perfect love casts out fear. The movement of the Holy Spirit in the heart of the believing woman should overcome passivity and strengthen leadership abilities. The objectivity of faith should replace subjective fancifulness and free the individual to fruitfully interact with reality.

Scripture inveighs against the type of negative male traits that have oppressed women:

Men are told not to lord it over others (1 Pet 5:3). They should not be proud (Rom 11:20; 2 Cor 10:5). Arrogance is blameworthy (Titus 1:7; 2 Tim 3:2; 1 Cor 4:18; 5:2). Selfish ambitions are to be curbed (2 Cor 12:20; Gal 5:20).

Other passages warn against being violent, lustful, shrewd, suspicious and rash.

"In Christ there is neither Greek nor Jew, neither male nor female" (Gal 3:28). Women have always been considered spiritually equal to men in Church teaching:

All men are endowed with a rational soul and are created in God's image; they have the same nature and origin and, being redeemed by Christ, they enjoy the same divine calling and destiny; there is here a basic equality between all men and it must be given ever greater recognition.

Undoubtedly not all men are alike as regards physical capacity and intellectual and moral powers. But forms of social or cultural discrimination in basic personal rights on the grounds of sex, race, color, social conditions, language or religion must be curbed and eradicated as incompatible with God's design. It is regrettable that these basic personal rights are not yet being respected everywhere, as is the case with women who are denied the chance freely to choose a husband, or a state of life, or to have access to the same educational and cultural benefits as are available to men (Flannery 1975, 929; *The Church in the Modern World*, 29).

The woman's strength in Christ begins at the very center of her desire to love and be loved:

It is the deepest desire of a woman's heart to surrender itself lovingly to another, to be wholly his and to possess him wholly. This is at the root of her tendency toward the personal and the whole, which seems to us the specifically feminine characteristic. Where this total surrender is made to a human being, it is a perverted self-surrender that enslaves her, and implies at the same time an unjustified demand that no human being can fulfill. Only God can receive the complete surrender of a person, and in such a way that she will not lose, but gain her soul. And only God can give himself to a human being in such a way that he will fulfill its whole being while losing nothing of his own. Hence the total surrender which is the principle of the religious [consecrated] life is at the same time the only possible adequate fulfillment of woman's desire (Stein 1956, 169).

Although single and married women make this surrender in a different manner than their consecrated sisters, it is nonetheless true that Christ must be first before others, so that he has room to fill our deepest longings.

We come to him each day in prayer and in the sacraments so that he can give himself to us. And his presence brings with it holy strength and true liberation.

The famous "Magnificat", which Mary sings in exaltation about her role as mother of the Messiah, overflows with spontaneity, strength and faith:

My soul magnifies the Lord and my spirit exults in God
  my Savior
For he has regarded the lowliness of his handmaid
For behold, all generations will call me blessed
For he that is mighty has done great things
and holy is his name. . . .
He has scattered the proud in the conceit of their hearts
The mighty he has cast down from their thrones
and he has exalted the humble

He has filled the hungry with good things
The rich he has sent empty away.

(Lk 1:46–53)

The women saints are brave, bold and true leaders, who are devoted to the Faith; think of Joan of Arc and Catherine of Siena, for example. Even the "quieter" saints have been enormously influential because of the power of their spiritual courage—Jane Frances de Chantal, Thérèse of Lisieux, Elizabeth Ann Seton. No conventional roles for women in the society of their times could hold them back from fidelity to the inspirations of the Holy Spirit.

Mother Frances Cabrini, the first American citizen to be canonized, had a terror of the sea. Yet moved by the Spirit, she had the courage to take a ship from Italy to America to tend to the needs of her fellow immigrants, who were losing the Faith due to lack of the ministry of those who could speak Italian.

Many women mystics have written about their experiences of God. However, it was the combination of ecstasy with clarity of thought shown by Saints Catherine of Siena and Teresa of Avila which led to their being proclaimed Doctors of the Church.

Blessed Maria Taigi, wife of an Italian porter, loving mother of many children, instructed Cardinals with the words the Lord sent her in prophecy.

What delights me in reading the lives of the women saints is their individuality. No two are alike. All were freed from the shackles of convention and from the rigidity of roles by the strength of the Spirit within them.

Once when trying desperately to figure out how to be

assertive yet not aggressive, I realized that when I am truly in tune with the Holy Spirit then I am sure I am doing the right thing, and I can fight for it valiantly without becoming threatened or abrasive. "God and I constitute a majority", as the humorous adage has it.

"Grace perfects nature"; it does not destroy it. Women's energies, which might go into manipulation, possessiveness or seduction, are channeled by the Spirit into charming delicacy in the expression of love of neighbor, sincere openness in prayer and surrender of beloved ones into the hands of God, who loves them more than she can.

When I am doing God's will in faith, I have peace and peace strengthens me to be feminine and free. If we strive for the good rather than our own selfish aims, then a loving energy spills over from the feminine into the free, and from the free back into the feminine.

"We learn . . . to yield to a will that moves in us but is not our own, that does not snuff out our own will, but moves ours strongly into accord with its own" (Ulanov 1981, 26). Ann Ulanov views the experience of being a woman who is in touch with a larger reality, God, not as nullifying her personal identity, but as enlarging it.

It seems, however, that not all Christian women experience faith as lived in the Church as a source of freedom. Some Christian feminists claim that the use of masculinely oriented language makes women feel second class. Patriarchal structures denying leadership roles for women keep them in a subservient position. Dogmatic formulations sometimes deny freedoms women should enjoy particularly in the area of "reproductive" freedom.

Here are some references to Christian feminists stressing such points (later to be critiqued):

On Inclusive Language

Recently the National Council of Churches voted to change Scripture readings in Church services so that God might be addressed as Father and Mother. An optional lectionary will remove the pronoun "He" in reference to God and Jesus will be called "Child" rather than "Son" of God.

Some Roman Catholic women feel alienated by what is erroneously termed exclusive language even though they are aware that the intent is not discriminatory.

"The generic use of man as inclusive of woman does not always work, because too often when we hear *man* we understand male person not human person. . . . When we only refer to God as masculine, we render invisible that dimension of the divine best expressed by feminine images" (Riley 1985, 29).

Rosemary Reuther, in the article "Feminist Theology and Spirituality" in *Christian Feminism: Visions of a New Humanity* (San Francisco, 1984), proposes calling God "She/he" or the "God-ess".

Some want to see patriarchal words such as "Lord" and "Judge" eliminated in favor of "Creator" and "Source".

On Leadership of Women in the Church

Three main areas of consideration in leadership are non-ordained pastoral ministry, the diaconate and the priesthood. The following illustrate the broad spectrum of feminist positions.

Many Christian women as well as those identified as Christian feminists would like to see more women in pastoral, advisory and decision-making roles in the

Church. Verbal and monetary appreciation should be expressed for such ministry. In many areas where there is a shortage of priests, women have assumed pastoral leadership.

The role of deaconess as a sacramental ministry has been widely recommended by women and also by bishops such as the German Episcopate (1981).

The exclusion of altar girls by canon law seems symptomatic of discriminatory attitudes. (See report of the World Union of Catholic Women's Organizations, in *Origins*, May 2, 1985.) Christian feminists take hope from such theological statements as these:

"The New Testament evidence, while not decisive by itself, points toward the admission of women to priestly ministry" (from a report of the Catholic Biblical Association of America, 1979).

There may be no sufficient evidence that the exclusion of women from the priesthood was a deliberate choice of Christ (see Karl Rahner *Theological Investigations XX* [1981] and *In Memory of Her* by Elisabeth Schussler-Fiorenza [1984]).

Some male priests who have recommended ordination of women consider their exclusion to be an instance of extreme ethical injustice. Women who leave the Roman Church in protest could be right.

Feminine base communities are often recommended as the center of Christian life for women, along with parallel participation in sexist institutional Churches for revolutionary purposes (see *Christian Feminism: Visions of a New Humanity*, edited by Judith L. Weidman [1984]).

In the Roman Catholic Church there is a Women's Ordination Conference in dialogue with the Bishops pressing for ordination as a right. Some women who are reportedly celebrating "Mass" already use feminist liturgies.

Research is being carried out by the Catholic Theological Society of America concerning the weight of arguments, pro and con, on women's ordination (see the research report published by the Catholic Theological Society of America [1978]). Sister Sara Butler, M.S.B.T., a member of this society and also a consultant to the U.S. Bishops' committee writing a pastoral on women, has made several summaries of these reflections. Key points to consider are whether the exclusion of women from priesthood in the early Church was based on the will of Christ or rather on cultural conditions. Is it not possible that considerations of equality and need outweigh an outmoded tradition?

Anthropological considerations based on theories of complementarity are judged by some to be invalid in the light of current findings.

Cannot a woman equally represent Christ since in Christ there is "neither male nor female"?

On Reproductive Freedom

When we look at the Church, we discover . . . the voice and experience of women have no access to decision-making processes of the Church, even in matters that directly relate to the quality of their own lives. Birth control is an example (from *In God's Image* by Maria Riley [1985, 24]).

Many Christian feminists simply take abortion for granted as a reproductive right (see *Christian Feminism: Visions of a New Humanity*).

In 1985 a furor was created when a number of Roman

Catholics were quoted in a prominent *New York Times* advertisement saying that they believed that there could be a plurality of views on abortion in the Church.

Truths and Falsehoods of Christian Feminism

The idea that Christian women cannot come into their own strengths as free women in Christ because of existing mind-sets and patterns in the Church is certainly false; yet the concerns of feminism should not be dismissed as having no basis whatever.

It seems that becoming aware of feminine images of God, while not proving that God is revealed equally as feminine and masculine, does help us to get in touch with this dimension, and is especially helpful for Christians who overemphasize God as power.

The need for more women in the ministry seems clear to me, especially since I am in this field as speaker, workshop director, retreat facilitator, professor at a seminary and consultant to Bishops. I have been very blessed by the ministry of women speakers, prophetesses, writers and counsellors.

Most women in ministry have to work in other areas to earn a living and do ministry on a volunteer or part-time basis. This is a shame since these women are full of zeal and energy for full-time roles in the Church.

I would welcome more education for Church men, religious and lay, on the problem of oppressive negative masculine traits such as cold, arrogant, smug and domineering behavior.

On the other hand, I have difficulty with many other Christian feminist concepts.

I believe that faith entails accepting revelation rather

than remaking religion in terms of secular and rationalistic ideals.

On the basis of reason it is hard to understand why God should reveal himself to a chosen race rather than making himself clearly present to all men.

"The God of Abraham, Isaac and Jacob" is not the God of the philosophers. He reveals himself as Lord and Father and not only as "Creator-Source". He enters the world as a Son, not as a daughter or a unisex robot or a two-sexed, twin birth.

For this reason I see efforts to change language about God as misguided. The best book I have read on this subject is by a Protestant theologian, Donald G. Bloesch. In *Battle for the Trinity: The Debate over Inclusive God Language* (1985) Bloesch argues that changes in symbolic images of God amount to rewriting the Bible to substitute a religion of experience. He makes startling comparisons with the way German Christians during the Nazi period devised their own version of Christianity trying to "conserve what was abiding and reject what is stultifying, purging Christianity of its Jewish elements" (Bloesch, 69–88). Bloesch takes great exception to the gradual introduction of pagan symbols among some feminists. Here is a striking quotation from Ernest Bergmann, one of the German theologians identified by Bloesch: "I believe in the God of the German religion who is at work in nature, in the lofty human spirit and in the strength of his people. I believe in the helper, Christ, who is struggling for the noble human soul" (Bloesch 1985, 70).

I was struck by this analogy. I have begun to notice in feminist writings a similar infusion of a sort of nature religion into spirituality. By contrast I view the documents of Vatican II as demonstrating a wonderful balance between clear supernatural doctrine and authentic humanism and guiding revelation with prayerful appropriation.

Regarding ordination of women, here are the main views given by the Vatican in its *Declaration on the Question of the Admission of Women to the Ministerial Priesthood* (1976, 8–11).

Could the Church today depart from this attitude of Jesus and the Apostles, which has been considered normative by the whole of tradition up to our own day? Various arguments have been put forward in favor of a positive reply to this question, and these must now be examined.

It has been claimed in particular that the attitude of Jesus and the Apostles is explained by the influence of their milieu and their times. It is said that, if Jesus did not entrust to women and not even to his Mother a ministry assimilating them to the Twelve, it was because historical circumstances did not permit him to do so. No one, however, has ever proved—and it is clearly impossible to prove—that this attitude is inspired only by social and cultural reasons. As we have seen, an examination of the Gospels shows on the contrary that Jesus broke with the prejudices of the time, by widely contravening the discriminations practiced with regard to women. One therefore cannot maintain that, by not calling women to enter the group of the Apostles, Jesus was simply letting himself be guided by reasons of expediency. For all the more reason, social and cultural conditioning did not hold back the Apostles working in the Greek milieu, where the same forms of discrimination did not exist.

Another objection is based on the transitory character that some claim to see today in some of the prescriptions of Saint Paul concerning women, and upon the difficulties that some aspects of his teaching raise in this regard. But it must be noted that these ordinances, probably inspired by the customs of the period, concern scarcely more than disciplinary practices of minor importance, such as the obligation imposed on women to wear a veil on the head (1 Cor 11:2–16); such requirements no longer have a normative value. However, the Apostle's forbidding women "to speak" in the assemblies (see 1 Cor 14:34–35; 1 Tim 2:12) is of a different nature, and exegetes define its meaning in this way: Paul in no way opposes the right, which he elsewhere recognizes as possessed by women, to prophesy in the assembly (1 Cor 11:5); the prohibition solely concerns the official function of teaching in the Christian assembly. For Saint Paul this prescription is bound up with the divine plan of creation (1 Cor 11:7; Gen 2:18–24): it would be difficult to see in it the expression of a cultural fact. Nor should it be forgotten that we owe to Saint Paul one of the more vigorous texts in the New Testament on the fundamental equality of men and women, as children of God in Christ (see Gal 3:28). Therefore there is no reason for accusing him of prejudices against women, when we note the trust he shows toward them and the collaboration he asks of them in his apostolate.

But over and above these objections taken from the history of apostolic times, those who support the legitimacy of change in the matter turn to the Church's practice in her sacramental discipline. It has been noted, in our day especially, to what extent the Church is conscious of possessing a certain power over the sacraments, even though they were instituted by Christ. She has used this power down the centuries in order to determine their signs and the conditions of their administration: recent decisions by Popes Pius XII and Paul VI are proof of that. However, it must be emphasized that this power, which is a real one, has definite limits. As Pope Pius XII recalled:

"The Church has no power over the substance of the sacraments, that is to say, over what Christ the Lord, as the sources of Revelation bear witness, determined should be maintained in the sacramental sign." This was already the teaching of the Council of Trent, which declared: "In the Church there has always existed this power, that in the administration of the sacraments, provided that their substance remains unaltered, she can lay down or modify what she considers more fitting either for the benefit of those who receive them or for respect toward those same sacraments, according to varying circumstances, times or places."

Moreover, it must not be forgotten that the sacramental signs are not conventional ones. Not only is it true that, in many respects, they are natural signs because they respond to the deep symbolism of actions and things, but they are more than that; they are principally meant to link the person of every period to the supreme Event of the history of salvation, in order to enable that person to understand, through all the Bible's wealth of pedagogy and symbolism, what grace they signify and produce. For example, the sacrament of the Eucharist is not only a fraternal meal, but at the same time the memorial that makes present and actual Christ's sacrifice and his offering by the Church. Again, the priestly ministry is not just a pastoral service; it ensures the continuity of the functions entrusted by Christ to the Apostles and the continuity of the powers related to those functions. Adaptation to civilizations and times therefore cannot abolish, on essential points, the sacramental reference to constitutive events of Christianity and to Christ himself.

In the final analysis, it is the Church, through the voice of her Magisterium, that, in these various domains, decides what can change and what must remain immutable. When she judges that she cannot accept certain changes, it is because she knows she is bound by Christ's manner of acting. Her attitude, despite appearance, is therefore not one of archaism but of fidelity: it can be truly understood only in this light. The Church makes pronouncements in virtue of the Lord's promise and the presence of the Holy Spirit, in order to proclaim better the mystery of Christ and to safeguard and manifest the whole of its rich content.

This practice of the Church therefore has a normative character: in the fact of conferring priestly ordination only on men, it is a question of an unbroken tradition throughout the history of the Church, universal in the East and in the West, and alert to repress abuses immediately. This norm, based on Christ's example, has been and is still observed because it is considered to conform to God's plan for his Church.

In support of these positions it has been argued that it is dualistic to argue, as many Christian feminists do, that Jesus is primarily a person, not a male. The philosopher Mary F. Rousseau (1981) thinks that it is an essential part of human experience that others present themselves to us as male or female. To eliminate sexuality from the symbolic reenactment of the Sacrifice of the Cross in the Mass, the great nuptial act of the Bridegroom and the Bride, would have tremendously disruptive consequences.

I agree. As a convert from philosophical atheism, one of the most exciting features of Christianity for me was that *truth* became a *person*, divine yet visualizable. Reality was a drama not a syllogism.

I would find it as strange to have Christ played by a woman in the liturgical scenario—just because women now play other leadership roles—as to have Mary played by a man in a nativity scene to indicate that men are parents too.

As to the cultural argument, we should realize that God formed the culture of this people. He could have formed an alternate culture with matriarchal structures and been incarnated as a woman and later represented by woman priests. A rigorous distinction between culturally influenced teachings of Saint Paul and essential doctrines can be found in Stephen Clark's *Man and Woman in Christ*.

Exclusion of women priests, however, does not exclude women from other roles of leadership, as amply demonstrated in the history of the Church in her women witnesses, prophetesses, foundresses, doctors, teachers and ministers to the ill and the poor.

The question of ordaining deaconesses is hard to assess at this writing due to theological debate about the ordained and nonordained positions of deaconesses in the early Church. So I will refrain from commenting.

Christian feminists' concern with "reproductive freedom" contradicts the objective tenets of reason and faith. An incisive analysis of the shortcomings of Christian feminism in this and other areas can be found in the Christendom publication, "Christian Feminism" by Nancy Cross (1984). So-called Christian feminists are often women who seriously diverge from fundamental Christian truth by denying the Resurrection as a literal happening, questioning eternal life and the real presence in the Eucharist. In this light, it is not surprising that Christ's moral teachings also become subject to revision.

As I have tried to show through *Feminine, Free and Faithful*, a woman's sexuality is so bound up with the expression of her feminine nature that violations of it do her great damage.

Such departures from the way of the Lord as fornication, contraception, abortion and divorce also destroy masculinity.

As E. Michael Jones writes:

> When the institution of marriage is weakened, men react in ways that are sexually pathological. . . . Women are insecure, afraid they will not be provided for and so become incapable of giving up their jobs and having children. Men, in this situation, . . . begin to feel emasculated because of their lack of authority, most especially the authority which goes with fatherhood. As a result, they seek to prove their masculinity in other, pathological ways (Jones 1984, 5).

However, many Christians will need an entire conversion to the Lord before they can listen to his moral teachings as transmitted through the Holy Spirit.

I believe that the crucial factor is having such faith in Christ's promises that it is possible to accept suffering for the Kingdom in ways which touch on our hope for personal happiness. In this way, we come full circle to see how interlinked are the feminine, freedom and faithfulness.

The last section on freedom transfigured by faith is about Mary.

Mary, Our Mother

For the Christian woman, the most beautiful image of womanhood—feminine, free and faithful—will always be Mary, the Mother of God. Created perfectly without sin by God the Father, indwelt by the Holy Spirit and filled by Christ, the Son, she is both the dove, the feminine handmaid and the fire of the Magnificat.

Think of the courage of a woman ready to be stoned to death by her people in obedience to a message that could only have sounded insane to any person she might confide it to! Think of her trust in the midst of anguish, hearing that innocents would be put to death and women convulsed in misery as Herod sought her Son and gave the brutal command to murder all the young male babies of the region of Bethlehem! Think of her deep delight in sharing in the secrets of her Son's future mission, later telling of his hidden life, strengthening the apostles who would be going to martyrdom!

The dogmas about Mary, unfortunately too often symbolized in saccharine statues, are nonetheless strong in their imagery. She is the woman who will crush the serpent under her heel, for she is the Immaculate Conception. She was assumed into heaven where she continues to minister to the Church, to intercede for us, to come to us in apparitions as Bride of God and Mother of the people of God, so unsentimental as to demand of a soft generation the rigors of fasting and penance. Mother Mary pleads for the life of her children.

As Cardinal Ratzinger writes in his book *Daughter Zion*, "Woman . . . is the mother of all life. . . . In this way the undestroyed dignity and majesty of woman are expressed. She preserves the mystery of life, the power opposed to death; for death is like the power of nothingness, the antithesis of Yahweh, who is the creator of life and the God of the living" (Ratzinger 1983, 17).

And so we see in the image of Mary, an icon of all the positive feminine traits: receptivity, delicacy, warmth, empathy, purity, beauty. Yet she is also as strong, as wise, as true, as courageous, as any holy male saint.

In going through my notes for a book I wrote with

Sister Mary Neill, O.P.: *Bringing the Mother with You: Healing Meditations on the Mysteries of Mary*, I came upon a meditation I had made at that time. It still seems beautiful and so I insert it here:

> In every woman there is the longing to be Mary—a pure flame of the sun. A woman who is a bonfire can enkindle—Yes!—but cannot give sustained warmth and light to her children.
>
> Joseph holds the Mary in us still, that we may know God, make our assent to be the Christ-bearer. He, the first priest, protects his bride, builds the house around her, the Church, so that the onrushing evil forces should not prevail while the New Life is being born. When the Josephs become Judases, the Marys become Eves cast out of Eden, buried in Sheol.
>
> Oh, Lord Jesus, unwind the shroud and resurrect your Church. Our Lady of Guadalupe—sublime stillness of the sun, intense enough to char your impress through our human cloaks, intercede for us.

And I hear Mary answering that prayer of mine, for she is the promise of our own celestial joy when we shall be feminine and free in the eternal kingdom—in the words of Zephaniah:

> Sing aloud, O daughter of Zion;
> shout, O Israel!
> The Lord, your God, is in your midst,
> he will rejoice over you with gladness,
> he will renew you with his love;
> he will exult over you with loud singing,
> as on a day of festival (Zeph 3:14–17).

Healing Exercises

Here are some ways you might choose to make the ideas in this chapter on freedom more personal to you:

1. Ask yourself when you have felt most free as a woman?

2. Read some of these Scriptures about aspects of freedom and ponder their message:

courageous: Josh 1:9; 1 Chron 19:13; Ps 27; Lam 1:6; Jn 11:16; 2 Cor 6:4–10. Making the Stations of the Cross can give us courage as we realize how much Jesus suffered.

leading: Meditating on the life of David, the Prophets and Christ, we can see how they take the lead rather than follow societal patterns.

strong: Song 8:6; 1 Kings 2:1–2; Ps 24:8; Ps 136:12; Prov 23:11; Is 35:3–4; Lk 1:80; Rom 4:20; Eph 6:10–20.

just: Dt 33:21; Ps 111:1–8; Ps 145:17; Prov 12:5; Is 11:1–5; Is 61:8; Mt 1:19; Jn 5:30; Phil 4:8.

self-controlled: Prov 25:28; 1 Cor 7:5; 1 Cor 9:25; Gal 5:16–25; 2 Tim 1:7; 2 Pet 1:6; Titus 1:8.

3. Go through the list of traits associated with freedom (p. 65). Thank God for those positive ones you checked. Look at any negative ones that are yours and pray for healing of these as you explore their roots.

4. Have you ever been oppressed by rigidity in feminine roles or by masculine rejection of your equality? If so, can you forgive those who have hurt you? Pray for greater freedom and strength of character.

5. If you have sinned because of selfishness in pursuing your own fulfillment, you can repent and receive Christ's forgiveness in prayer and confession.

6. Meditate on the lives of Mary and other women saints for inspiration and intercession.

A Creed for Christian Women

I believe that God, the Father, created me
a *person: human, spiritual, immortal*
  — not a doll
  — not a sex object
  — not a slave
a *feminine person*
  — because God thought that my unique soul
    could best express itself as feminine
with *a beautiful feminine body*
  — to be clothed according to its shape
  — to be joined in overflowing eternal love to my
    spouse
    or
  — to be consecrated to himself in the mystical
    adventure of celibacy
    or
  — to remain hidden in him, if he wills, suspended
    in the world an unvowed free presence to all
capable of the *sacred act of transmitting his life to
creatures*, and therefore
  — not to be sold for gain
  — not to be bartered for passing pleasure,
    popularity or security
  — not to be nullified in creativity by contraceptive
    devices

— not to allow the killing of my own fruit
— but instead to be open to the life-giving seed of
my husband
bring forth new life
hold my babies close
feed them from my substance

I believe that God, the Son, as Jesus the Christ
*redeemed the image of God broken in by my destructive
conditioning of*
— family
— school
— the world at large
— the weight of our history
comes to heal me with the same absolute love he gave
to my ancient sisters
— Mary
announcing his love for me in his baptismal
kiss
— Martha
in daily familiar yet holy communion
— Mary Magdalen
in Penance's purging love embrace
teaches me *the path of sacrificial love*, never to seek
— self-fulfillment at the expense of the growth
of my sisters and brothers
— friendships of convenience
— the destruction of unwanted babies
— first place over husband and children
— first place over others at work
always to show loving kindness to others, and even
to myself, even when we are

— boxed-in, not "open"
— weak, not "strong"
— needy, not "beautiful"
inspires me to hope for
— understanding, emerging even out of friction
— reconciliation not divorce
— renewal not disaster
by the influx of his surprising, fresh, unpredictable,
infinite, flow of grace

I believe in God, the Holy Spirit
kindling the first flame of
— my God-given talents
— hidden crazy dreams
— my unending search for beauty
— my unquenchable longings for love
fanning the flame of my desire for being by
— the stunning loveliness of nature
— the fleeting promise of bliss in human love
— the sudden sweetness of small acts
— the amazing, forgiving, stable love of others
for me
— the haunting inspiration of the bold and holy
saints
raking the coals to recover the flame buried under
— limited images others had and have of me
— the put-downs of teachers and companions
— my own fear, apathy, failure and despair
that You and I and We might form *communities of
growth and love*
— at home
— at work

— in the world around
in spite of all our faults
on earth as it is in heaven

I believe in the mystical body of the Church because
in spite of
— our sins
— our ignorance
— our misery
we have preserved the vision of the immortal infinite
equality of all people female and male before God

we have taught the seeking not of his will or her will
but of God's will

we have known Christ's love pouring through us
not as me and you or she and he but as One Body

we have faith in him and proof in him that not
degradation, frustration, hate or despair, but *love*
will have the victory in the Eternal Kingdom.

and in Her, our Holy Church, I embrace my sisters
— longing, straining, seeking ones, and frustrated,
miserable, despairing ones who yet hope in God
— patient, holy martyrs of motherhood and irri-
table unhappy ones whom God blesses and
forgives
— mystical, celibate souls on fire with celestial
love and empty, saddened ones whom God
will one day fill to overflowing
together enfolded in the ample, azure mantle of
Our Lady of Liberation
Virgin, Mother, Saint

who accomplished the impossible
by total openness to God

Alleluia, Amen!

References

Abbott, Walter M. 1966. *The documents of Vatican II*. New York: Guild Press.

Abeel, Erica. 1981. The love and rape of Jean Harris. *Savvy* (April).

Andelin, Helen. 1980. *Fascinating womanhood*. New York: Bantam.

Bardwick, Judith. 1979. *In transition: how feminism, sexual liberation and the search for self-fulfillment have altered America*. New York: Holt, Rinehart and Winston.

Bloesch, Donald G. 1985. *Battle for the Trinity: the debate over inclusive God language*. Ann Arbor, Mich.: Servant Press.

Blumenfeld, Samuel. 1975. *The retreat from motherhood*. New Rochelle: Arlington House.

Caprio, Betsy. 1983. *The woman in the tower*. New York: The Paulist Press.

Catholic Theological Society of America (research report on women's ordination), Manhattan College, Bronx, N.Y. 10471.

Chervin, Ronda. 1979. *Christian ethics and your everyday life*. Los Angeles: S.C.R.C. Publications.

Chervin, Ronda, and Sr. Mary Neill. 1982. *Bringing the Mother with you: healing meditations on the mysteries of Mary*. New York: Seabury.

_____. 1980. *The woman's tale*. New York: Seabury.

Chesterton, G. K. 1942. *What's wrong with the world?*

Clark, Stephen B. 1980. *Man and woman in Christ*. Ann Arbor, Mich.: Servant Press.

Cross, Nancy. 1984. *Christian feminism*. Front Royal, Va.: Christendom Publications.

de Beauvoir, Simone. 1952. *The second sex*. Trans. by H. M. Parshley. New York: Alfred A. Knopf.

Declaration on the question of the admission of women to the ministerial priesthood. 1976. Washington, D.C.: United States Catholic Conference.

Durden-Smith, Jo. 1980. Male and female—why? *The Collegiate Career Woman* (Winter).

Flannery, Austin. 1975. *Vatican Council II: the Conciliar and postconciliar documents*. Northport, N.Y.: Costello Publishing Co.

Freidan, Betty. 1971. *The feminine mystique*. New York: Dell Books (first published in 1963. New York: Norton).

Gilligan, Carol. 1982. *In a different voice*. Cambridge: Harvard University Press.

Greer, Germaine. 1972. *The female eunuch*. New York: Bantam.

Harding, M. Esther. 1971. *Woman's mysteries*. New York: Harper Colophon. For a fascinating description of negative and positive ways of relating to the psychological impact of the menstrual cycle, see 64–83.

Hilberman, Elaine, M.D. 1980. Overview: the "wife beater's wife" reconsidered. *The American Journal of Psychiatry* 137 (November): 11.

John Paul II. 1981. *Familiaris Consortio*.

_____. 1981. *Original unity of man and woman*. Boston: Daughters of Saint Paul.

Jones, E. Michael. 1984. The asymmetry of the sexes. Affirmations.

Koedt, Anne, and Shulamith Firestone, eds., *Women's liberation, notes from the third year, an annual*. New York.

Lessing, Doris. 1970. *Children of violence*. New York: New American Library.

Lorde, Audre. 1978. *The black unicorn*. New York: W. W. Norton & Co.

Mahowald, Mary B. 1978. *Philosophy of women*. Indianapolis: Hackett Publishing Co. References to Mahowald excerpts apply to these works: Atkinson, Ti-Grace. Radical feminism. In *Amazon odyssey*; Aristotle. On the generation of animals. In *Generation of animals*. Trans. by A. Peck; Engels, Frederich. Origin of the family. In *Origin of the family, private property and the state*; Lenin, V. I. The woman question. In *The emancipation of women*; Mill, John Stuart. The subjection of women. In *On liberty*; Nietzsche, Friederich. Of womenkind, old and young. Of child and marriage. In *Thus spake Zarathustra*; Russell, Bertrand. The liberation of women. In *Marriage and morals*; Wollstonecraft, Mary. *A vindication of the rights of women*; Villar, Esther. What is woman? In *The manipulated man*.

Morgan, Marabel. 1975. *The total woman*. Old Tappan, N.J.: Fleming H. Revell.

Neill, Mary, Don Briel and Ronda Chervin. 1983. *How shall we find the Father?* New York: Seabury.

Plato. *Dialogues*. All editions of Plato's dialogues are numbered in sections in the same way. Relevant sections follow: *Symposium* 190–193; *Timaeus* 41d–42a, b, c; *Republic* 454e, 455d; *Laws* 802e, 721–722.

Rahner, Karl. 1981. *Theological investigations*, vol. 20. New York: Crossroad.

Ratzinger, Cardinal. 1983. *Daughter Zion*. Trans. by John McDermott. San Francisco: Ignatius Press.

Riley, Maria. 1985. *In God's image*. Kansas City, Mo.: Leaven Press.

Rossi, Alice S., ed. 1973. *The feminist papers*. New York: Columbia University Press.

Roszak, Betty and Theodore Roszak, eds. *Masculine / Feminine*. 1969. New York: Harper Colophon Books.

Rousseau, Mary F. 1981. Theological trends: the ordination of women; a philosopher's viewpoint. *The Way* 21 (July).

Sartre, Jean-Paul. 1949. *No exit and three other plays*. Trans. by L. Abel. New York: Vintage Books.

_____. 1957. *Being and nothingness*. Trans. by H. E. Barnes. London: McThuen.

Sayers, Dorothy. 1960. *Gaudy night*. New York: Harper and Row.

Schussler-Fiorenza, Elisabeth. 1984. *In memory of her*. New York: Crossroad.

Stein, Edith. 1956. *The writings of Edith Stein*. London: Peters Owen.

Stern, Karl. 1965. *The flight from woman*. New York: Farrar, Straus and Giroux.

Tiger, Lionel and Robin Fox. 1971. *The imperial animal*. New York: Holt, Rinehart and Winston.

Ulanov, Ann Belford. 1981. *Receiving woman*. Philadelphia: The Westminster Press.

Vilar, Esther. 1972. *The manipulated man*. New York: Farrar, Straus and Giroux. See especially 13–21.

von Balthasar, Hans Urs. 1981. Ephesians 5:21–33 and Humanae vitae: a meditation. In *Christian married love*, ed. Raymond Dennehy. San Francisco: Ignatius Press.

von Hildebrand, Dietrich. 1965. *Man and woman*. Chicago: Franciscan Herald Press.

_____. 1984. *Marriage*. Manchester, N.H.: Sophia Institute Press.

von Le Fort, Gertrude. 1962. *The eternal woman*. Trans. by Placid Jordan. Milwaukee: Bruce Publishing Co.

Weidman, Judith L., ed. 1984. *Christian feminism*. San Francisco: Harper and Row.

Wojtyla, Karol. 1981. *Love and responsibility*. Trans. by H. T. Willets. New York: Farrar, Straus and Giroux.